Wildlife Protection, Destruction and Extinction

Are Animals in Zoos Rather Conspicuous Than Endangered?

WILDLIFE PROTECTION, DESTRUCTION AND EXTINCTION

International Illegal Trade in Wildlife
Liana Sun Wyler and Pervaze A. Sheikh
2008. ISBN: 978-1-60456-757-1

Fishing, Hunting, and Wildlife Associated Recreation
Dustin N. Worley (Editor)
2009. ISBN: 978-1-60692-128-9

Wildlife: Destruction, Conservation and Biodiversity
John D. Harris and Paul L. Brown (Editors)
2009. ISBN: 978-1-60692-974-2

Wildlife Refuges: Factors and Concerns about Future Sustainability
Earl B. Taylor (Editor)
2010. ISBN: 978-1-60692-683-3

National Parks: Biodiversity, Conservation and Tourism
Angus O'Reilly and Doran Murphy (Editors)
2010. ISBN: 978-1-60741-465-0

Protecting Marine Mammals
Marielle de Vries (Editor)
2010. ISBN: 978-1-60741-569-5

National Parks and Rivers: Background, Protection and Use Issues
Yolanda A. Reddy (Editor)
2009. ISBN: 978-1-60741-801-6

Protection at the Wildlife - Urban Interface
Ernesto Di Bello (Editor)
2010. ISBN: 978-1-60876-093-0

Conservation Research in Uganda's Forests:
A Review of Site History, Research, and Use of Research
in Uganda's Forest Parks and Budongo Forest Reserve
William Olupot and Andrew J. Plumptre
2010. ISBN: 978-1-60876-577-5

Conservation Research in Uganda's Savannas:
A Review of Park History, Applied Research, and
Application of Research to Park Management
William Olupot, Luke Parry, Michelle Gunness and Andrew J. Plumptre
2010. ISBN: 978-1-60876-575-1

Biology, Evolution and Conservation of River Dolphins
within South America and Asia
Manuel Ruiz-Garcia and Joseph Mark Shostell (Editors)
2010. ISBN: 978-1-60876-633-8

National Parks: Vegetation, Wildlife and Threats
Grazia Polisciano and Olmo Farina (Editors)
2010. ISBN: 978-1-60876-742-7

Are Animals in Zoos Rather Conspicuous Than Endangered?
Frynta, D., Marešová, J., Landová, E., Lišková, S., Šimková,
O., Tichá, I., Zelenková, M., and Fuchs, R.
2010. ISBN: 978-1-61668-234-7

Are Animals in Zoos Rather Conspicuous Than Endangered?
Frynta, D., Marešová, J., Landová, E., Lišková, S., Šimková,
O., Tichá, I., Zelenková, M., and Fuchs, R.
2010. ISBN: 978-1-61668-499-0 (E-book)

WILDLIFE PROTECTION, DESTRUCTION AND EXTINCTION

ARE ANIMALS IN ZOOS RATHER CONSPICUOUS THAN ENDANGERED?

D. FRYNTA
J. MAREŠOVÁ
E. LANDOVÁ
S. LIŠKOVÁ
O. ŠIMKOVÁ
I. TICHÁ
M. ZELENKOVÁ
AND
R. FUCHS

Nova Science Publishers, Inc.
New York

Copyright © 2010 by Nova Science Publishers, Inc.

All rights reserved. No part of this book may be reproduced, stored in a retrieval system or transmitted in any form or by any means: electronic, electrostatic, magnetic, tape, mechanical photocopying, recording or otherwise without the written permission of the Publisher.

For permission to use material from this book please contact us:
Telephone 631-231-7269; Fax 631-231-8175
Web Site: http://www.novapublishers.com

NOTICE TO THE READER

The Publisher has taken reasonable care in the preparation of this book, but makes no expressed or implied warranty of any kind and assumes no responsibility for any errors or omissions. No liability is assumed for incidental or consequential damages in connection with or arising out of information contained in this book. The Publisher shall not be liable for any special, consequential, or exemplary damages resulting, in whole or in part, from the readers' use of, or reliance upon, this material. Any parts of this book based on government reports are so indicated and copyright is claimed for those parts to the extent applicable to compilations of such works.

Independent verification should be sought for any data, advice or recommendations contained in this book. In addition, no responsibility is assumed by the publisher for any injury and/or damage to persons or property arising from any methods, products, instructions, ideas or otherwise contained in this publication.

This publication is designed to provide accurate and authoritative information with regard to the subject matter covered herein. It is sold with the clear understanding that the Publisher is not engaged in rendering legal or any other professional services. If legal or any other expert assistance is required, the services of a competent person should be sought. FROM A DECLARATION OF PARTICIPANTS JOINTLY ADOPTED BY A COMMITTEE OF THE AMERICAN BAR ASSOCIATION AND A COMMITTEE OF PUBLISHERS.

LIBRARY OF CONGRESS CATALOGING-IN-PUBLICATION DATA

Available Upon Request

ISBN : 978-1-61668-234-7

Published by Nova Science Publishers, Inc. ✛ New York

CONTENTS

Preface		**ix**
Introduction		**xi**
Chapter 1	Data Sources and Testing Procedures	**1**
Chapter 2	Representation of Vertebrate Classes in Zoos	**3**
Chapter 3	Size of Captive Populations	**7**
Chapter 4	Relative Representation of Endangered Species	**11**
Chapter 5	Effects of Perceived Attractiveness and Body Size among Related Species	**15**
Chapter 6	Effects of Perceived Attractiveness and Body Size on Higher Taxonomic Scale	**21**
Chapter 7	Preferred Species and Characters	**39**
Conclusion		**53**
About the Authors		**63**
Index		**65**

PREFACE

The chapter challenges the assumption that humans generally treat all animal species equally according to their need of conservation. We have reviewed recent studies suggesting that humans show strong preferences toward particular animal species/taxa and are willing to protect them more than others. Such understanding of human preferences is an important part of conservation strategies.

The main body of the chapter is based on original data analyses performed separately for main reptile, bird and mammalian taxa. The representation of animal taxa in zoos and the sizes of zoo populations are reviewed. Human preferences to particular species and/or families were examined directly by presenting their pictures to the respondents. The results showed that factors affecting human aesthetic preferences toward particular species differ among higher taxonomic groups. We concluded that animal attractiveness (both body size and beauty itself) influences human effort devoted to ex situ breeding projects more than inclusion in Red book lists. Special attention has to be paid to less preferred, but endangered species. Fortunately, the highly preferred species are present in almost every family and also among threatened species. Thus, the zoos can replace preferred but common species by endangered one that meets both, conservation as well as visitor's aesthetic criteria.

INTRODUCTION

Captive breeding has enabled survival of numerous species facing extinction. The stories of such species as California condor (*Gymnogyps californianus*), Hawaiian goose (*Branta sandvicensis*), black-footed ferret (*Mustela nigripes*), Guam rail (*Gallirallus owstoni*), Lord Howe Island woodhen (*Gallirallus sylvestris*), golden lion tamarin (*Leonthopithecus rosalia*), European bison (*Bos bonasus*), addax (*Addax naomaculatus*), scimitar-horned oryx (*Oryx dammah*), Arabian oryx (*Oryx leocoryx*), southern white rhino (*Ceratotherium simum simum*) or Przewalski's horse (*Equus przewalskii*) are well-known textbook examples (cf. Frankham et al. 2002, Frankham 2008). Many of these species were saved owing to few individuals unintentionally kept in various zoos, private farms and circuses. At the time of the crisis, these animals became founders of rescue breeding programs. Nowadays the proportion of potentially endangered species is rapidly increasing and in fact no species is actually safe from possible disaster (Wilson et al. 2002). Thus the maintenance of captive populations is a form of survival insurance.

Some reintroduction programs were fairly successful (e.g., Denton et al. 1997, Brighsmith et al. 2005, White et al.2005, Bertolero et al. 2007, Brown et al. 2007, but see Price and Fa 2007). Nevertheless, the value of zoo populations as a source for future reintroduction may be questioned (e.g., Jule et al. 2008). Captive populations are affected by unintended behavioral (McDougall et al. 2006), morphological (O'Regan and Kitchener 2005, Connolly and Cree 2008) and genetic adaptations (Frankham 2008) to captivity. Most damaging are usually the loose of genetic variation and inbreeding (for review see Frankham et al. 2002). However, these problems as well as those associated with obtaining enough individuals for successful reintroduction event may be avoided by keeping source populations in sufficient numbers (i.e., hundreds or thousands specimens).

It is, however, not self-evident that any endangered species will be kept in sufficient numbers. Zoos are luxury hotels in the world full of animal refugees. Consequently, there is an excess of species in need and accommodation capacity is strictly limited (Soulé 1986, Wilson 1992, Tudge 1995). Moreover, new zoo exhibits tend to be larger and support markedly fewer individuals than the older ones (Baker 2007) as legal standards of welfare and veterinary care become more and more strict. As a result of these requirements the costs of keeping animals tend to gradually rise. This further escalates competition among animal species for ex situ breeding programs and increases the role of human decision making (Cohn 1992). The winners may be the species that satisfy human aesthetic and emotional requirements, rather than those most vulnerable. Moreover, fashon may further enhance risky fluctuations in captive populations of endangered species in a similar manner as reported in breeds of domestic dogs (Herzog et al. 2004).

Thorough analysis of reintroduction projects (Seddon et al. 2005) demonstrated apparent taxonomic bias, e.g., some attractive vertebrate taxa as mammals (especially artiodactyls and carnivores) and birds (anseriforms, falconiforms, gruiforms and galliforms) are overrepresented. As a result, species composition of future biota is more and more affected by an artificial species selection.

Animals have been an integral component of the human environment and culture from the very beginning of our species. Even illiterate hunter-gatherers were able to name and categorize animal species in a very similar way as contemporary scientists (Berlin 1992). Evolutionary psychologists suggest that our mind is evolutionarily prepared to respond to animal stimuli (Barkow et al. 1992). There is an innate predisposition to easily learn fear of snakes and spiders (Davey et al. 1998), and on the other hand, people experience positive emotions toward other taxa. It is not accidental that large herbivores, domestic animals and birds frequently occurred in paintings since the Pleistocene (Lewis-Williams 2002, Guthrie 2005) up to the Modern Age (Baenninger 1988, Barkow et al. 1992). Both positive and negative emotions raise human interest in the particular species. It should be emphasized that the vast majority of species are inevitably neglected by us. Anthropologists and ethnobiologists demonstrated in tribal societies that the number of generic names, each representing an independent concept of an animal, usually does not exceed 500 units (for a review see Berlin 1992). Thus our mental capacity devoted to animals is scant in view of the worldwide diversity of the vertebrate genera. Consequently, the endangered species compete with one another for our attention that may help them by providing financial and political support for conservation projects.

Introduction

As a rule, distribution of any conservation effort and willingness to support varies greatly from species to species. Funding decisions by FWS (Federal Wildlife Service) are not related to a species recovery priority rank (Simon et al. 1995). The U.S. federal government's protection and spending decisions concerning individual species are based more on "visceral" characteristics of the species (i.e. physical size and the degree to which the species is considered to be a "higher form of life") than on "scientific" ones (i.e. degree of endangerment and "taxonomic uniqueness") (Metrick & Weitzman 1996). Incredibly, a 10% increase in body length is associated with an 8.6% rise in funding. Sometimes, human willingness to protect a species may even negatively correlate with the degree of endangerment. Metrick and Weitzman (1998) reported this phenomenon in public comments on the changes in the Red List. There is more public support for saving species perceived as attractive, larger in size (Gunnthorsdottir 2001) and resembling humans (Samples et al. 1986).

Animal taxa differ also in its social construction and political power (expressed as, e.g., number of NGOs supporting particular animals). Birds receive the highest public support among vertebrates; however, mammals and fish also belong to "advantaged" taxa. In contrast, amphibians and reptiles (except turtles and tortoises) receive almost no support (Czech et al. 1998, see also Kellert 1985).

Humans are able to differentiate between attractive and unattractive animals, e.g., cat or tiger faces from early childhod (Quinn et al. 2008). Interestingly, nearly all species reported by respondents as most preferred are mammals (Morris 1967). Although, human-animal relationships in zoos are more complex phenomenon (Hosey 2008), popularity of zoo animals may be successfully explained by simple traits as body size (Ward et al. 1998). Plethora additional hypotheses were proposed (e.g., Morris 1967) to explain differential attractiveness of animal species for humans: most studied were the effects of juvenile body proportions (Gould 1979, Pittenger 1990), form close to average appearance (Halberstadt and Rhodes 2003) and conspicuous coloration (e.g., Van Hook 1997, Stokes 2007).

Although perceived attractiveness of animal species is easy to quantify and its potential consequences for conservation practice are fundamental, little attention has been paid to these issues so far. Moreover, existing studies usually suffer from comparisons among unrelated groups of animals and small number of compared species. Quantitative studies carried out on a finer taxonomic scale are therefore needed.

Recently we studied the influence of factors putatively enhancing sensory stimulation of human observers (i.e., zoo visitors and/or keepers) on ex situ conservation efforts. We analyzed worldwide zoo populations of boas and pythons; we have found strong positive effects of perceived attractiveness on the zoo population size of the species worldwide (Marešová and Frynta 2008).

Although we are aware of that local culture may affect human preferences toward animal species, an elementary cross-cultural agreement could be reasonably expected. This assumption derived from evolutionary psychological theory (Barkow et al. 1992) should, however, be subjected to further testing. Our preliminary data reveal surprisingly close correspondence between rankings of snake species by people from such different cultures as are those in Europe and Papua New Guinea (Marešová, Krása and Frynta, in press).

In this chapter we examine population sizes of animals in zoos worldwide. We focus on three classes of terrestrial vertebrates (Amniota): reptiles, birds and mammals, and analyze factors affecting representation of these animals in zoos. Besides taxonomic bias (uneven representation of particular taxa) and representation of endangered species, we paid special attention to body size and perceived attractiveness of zoo animals.

Chapter 1

DATA SOURCES AND TESTING PROCEDURES

To avoid problems with uncertain nomenclature and taxonomy, we used the following species lists which are nowadays widely accepted by vertebrate zoologists: Wilson and Reeder (2005, available on http://nmnhgoph.si.edu/msw/) for mammals, Masi (1996, available on http://www.scricciolo.com/ classificazione/sibley's_index.htm) and The BirdLife Checklist (The BirdLife Taxonomic Working Group (BTWG), 2008; based mainly on Sibley and Monroe (1990, 1993); available on http://www.birdlife.org/datazone/species/ taxonomy.html) for birds and The TIGR Reptile Database for reptiles (Uetz et al. 2008; available on http://www.reptile-database.org). The extinct and domestic animals (dog, cat, cow, horse, goat, sheep, camels, lamas, pig, laboratory mouse, rat, guinea pig, hen, turkey, goose and duck) were excluded, although some of them may be viewed as endangered (Taberlet et al. 2008). The IUCN status of all species was obtained from the official IUCN website (IUCN 2008; http://www.iucnredlist.org). The above species lists do not match one another exactly and also their agreement with taxonomies used by zoos is limited. To avoid mistakes we resolved these disparities ad hoc, and therefore the total numbers of species in particular taxa may a bit deviate from that found in the original databases.

The population size of each species in worldwide zoo collections was obtained from The International Species Information System database (ISIS, http:// www.isis.org, downloaded on 1 January 2008). It seems to be the only relevant public source covering approximately 730 zoos and aquaria all over the world.

It may be argued that the database does not include all keepers as some local zoos as well as private breeders are not comprised. However, we consider the institutions participating in ISIS to be the most important since they support a much larger number of animals, at least in the case of some larger species, compared with that kept by the other breeders. Last but not least, breeding programs of these credible institutions are well coordinated and attract the attention of the general public and the media, thus helping the selected species gain additional support. The number of individuals kept in zoos provides therefore a good estimate of the conservation efforts.

To assess human preferences towards animal species, we asked our respondents (mostly students from various faculties of the Charles University in Prague) to sort particular sets of pictures and rank the animals according to the perceived aesthetic attractiveness (beauty) following method of Marešova and Frynta (2008).

We carried out these analyses at two different levels: (1) Species, by comparing particular species within a family (pythons and boas – Boidae, pheasants – Phasianidae, antelopes and allies – Bovidae) or an order (turtles – Testudines); (2) higher taxa, by comparing families or sufamilies, each represented by a randomly selected species (see under Effects of perceived attractiveness and body size on higher taxonomic scale; Table 3).

For statistical analyses we used STATISTICA 6.0, StatSoft Inc. (2001). Prior the statistical analyses, the data were normalized when necessary; population and body sizes were log-transformed, while relative ranks of pictures were square-root arcsin transformed. Either GLM models or Multiple Linear Regression were applied. The agreement in ranking the pictures was visualized by Principal Component Analysis (PCA). The percentage of explained variability by the first principle component (PC1) was used to quantify the congruence among the respondents.

Chapter 2

REPRESENTATION OF VERTEBRATE CLASSES IN ZOOS

It has been previously demonstrated that the vertebrate species kept in zoos are unequally distributed among higher taxa. Mammals and birds are obviously overrepresented while amphibians and fishes tend to be underrepresented (e.g., Price and Fa 2007, Leader-Williams 2007). Nevertheless, the differential representation of vertebrate taxa in the worldwide zoo population is worth further analyses. This is an obligatory step towards understanding the underlying processes that control the efficiency of ex situ conservation.

Even a first glance at the data (Table 1) is eloquent. The numbers of species kept in zoos are surprisingly high. As many as 1154 reptile, 2337 bird, and 990 mammalian species, representing 13.4%, 24.3%, and 18.5% of non-extinct species of these groups, respectively are listed among the zoo population.

The total numbers of individuals kept in zoos are about the same for birds and mammals (200 and 152 thousand, respectively), while the corresponding figure is nearly three times lower for reptiles (67 thousands). When the number of individuals kept in zoos was scaled to the total number of living species of the given class, the difference was even more evident. In zoos, there are just 7.80 reptiles, but 20.74 birds and even 28.45 mammals per total number of living species. Only a small portion of this difference may be attributed to the fact that reptiles (as well as amphibians and fishes) are more frequently kept in small zoos and private collections which are not covered by the ISIS database. As mammals and birds are in general more active, possess higher metabolism (Schmidt-Nielsen 1984), need larger spaces and more keeper's care than reptiles and other cold-blooded vertebrates, their clear overrepresentation in zoos is in a strong contradiction to the elevated costs of keeping them (see also Balmford 2000).

Obviously, this phenomenon reflects some kind of human preference in favor of these warm-blooded animals.

Table 1. Representation of reptiles, birds and mammals in zoos.

Class:	Reptiles	Birds	Mammals
number of living species	8602	9627	5353
number of individuals in zoos	67073	199686	152314
number of species kept in zoos	1154	2337	990
number of species with zoo population size over 50	247	634	416
number of species with zoo population size over 500	28	80	79
number of zoo individuals per living species	7.8	20.7	28.5
% zoo species out of all living species	13.4	24.3	18.5
% species with zoo population size over 50 out of all living species	2.9	6.6	7.8
% species with zoo population size over 500 out of all living species	0.3	0.8	1.5
% zoo species with population size over 50 out of all zoo species	21.4	27.1	42.0
% zoo species with population size over 500 out of all zoo species	2.4	3.4	8.0
number of individuals in zoos/ n of species kept in zoos	58.1	85.5	153.9
mean size of zoo population computed from log-transformed data	12.6	14.5	30.3
median	12	13	34.5
lower quartile	3	3	6
upper quartile	39	57	141
H' (Index of diversity, Shannon and Wiener 1963)	5.543	6.152	5.671
J' (Index of equitability, Sheldon 1969)	0.786	0.793	0.822
H'/H'max (real biodiversity in zoos/maximal possible biodiversity)	0.612	0.671	0.660

We understand the network of zoos (cf. Field and Dickie 2007) as a specific habitat supporting specific synusy of the animals that may be studied by the methods adopted from the ecology of communities. We applied the standard indices of species diversity (H'; Shannon 1963; natural logarithms were used for the computations) and equitability (J'; Pielou 1966, Sheldon 1969). The former index increases with increasing number of species as well as with increasing equitability of their representation in the synusy (worldwide zoo network in our case). The latter one (ranging from 0 to 1) quantifies only the equitability component of diversity and is thus independent on the number of species. It is the ratio between the observed H' and maximum theoretical value of H' computed for the observed number of species in a given sample. As the equitability assessed by J' omits the species which are not present in zoos by at least one individual, we computed an additional modified index of equitability (I) as the ratio between H' and the maximum theoretical H' computed for the total number of species in the taxon (class).

In general, the values of all the three indices were fairly similar among the studied classes of vertebrates. From this it follows that zoos are not extremely selective with respect to the vertebrate classes. There are, however, some remarkable differences. Birds as a specious group with the highest number of zoo species have a higher index of diversity (H'=6.15) than less specious mammals (5.67) and reptiles (5.54). Surprisingly, our modified index of equitability also suggests that zoos support higher species diversity in the case of birds (I=0.671) and mammals (0.660), than in reptiles (0.612). In contrast, the standard index of equitability was somewhat higher in mammals (J'=0.822) than in birds (0.793) and reptiles (0.786). Thus, the biodiversity of warm bloodied vertebrates is better represented in zoos than that of reptiles, but the main reasons clearly differ between birds and mammals. These are high number of bird species kept in zoos, while fairly equal size of captive populations in the case of mammals.

Chapter 3

SIZE OF CAPTIVE POPULATIONS

The worldwide zoo populations of most vertebrate species are extremely small (Table 1). Zoos keep on average 58, 85 and 154 individuals per one reptile, bird and mammalian species occurred in zoos, respectively. These figures are, however, much higher than those typical for zoo species of these taxa. It is due to log-normal distribution of zoo population sizes. When this statistical distribution is taken into account, the respective means decrease to 12.6, 14.5 and 30.3. One half of the reptile, bird and mammalian species have the worldwide zoo population smaller than median values 12, 13, and 34.5, respectively. Populations of such sizes are obviously not sustainable and stochastic demographic and genetic processes lead to their extinction or genetic degradation within a few generations nearly inevitably (Frankham et al. 2002) even in such improbable case that all kept animals take part in reproduction. It is really doubtful whether perpetuation of such small populations in captivity may play any beneficial role in ex situ conservation except attracting the public and providing an opportunity for zoo staff training and accumulation of skills in how to keep and breed a given species (for the role of zoos in conservation education see Sterling et al. 2007).

On the other hand, some successful rescue breeding projects started with only handful captive specimens. Sometimes, small number of founders was enough even for reestablishment of free-ranging population (e.g., Taylor et al. 2005). This is in accord with population genetic theory suggesting a few (>10) unrelated individuals of diploid species contain vast majority of the overall genetic variation of the large source population. Therefore, from purely genetic perspective even narrow bottlenecks followed by a rapid restoration of the population size are not as risky as prolonged maintenance of low or moderate population size (Frankham et al. 2002). Thus presence of just a few unrelated individuals in zoos may occasionally save the species if captive population is immediately expanded when necessary, e.g., after unexpected crisis of the wild populations (but see Hale and Briskie 2007 for negative effects of bottlenecking). The prerequisite that the founding animals have to be unrelated says in another words either obtained from nature or from another large captive population. This, however, requires blurring boundaries between captive and wild populations (Dickie et al. 2007).

Fundamental theory of population ecology suggests that removal of handful individuals have usually no deleterious effect on wild populations. In steady-state or increasing populations, the removed individuals are easily replaced by those born and/or survived due to relaxation of density dependent factors. Even in most declining populations, loose of few individuals does not matter. In spite of this, it is increasingly difficult to source animals from wild (Dickie et al. 2007). Administrative obstacles, usually resulting from misinterpretation and/or bureaucratic abuse of conservation legislation (Holst and Dickie 2007) prevent zoos to exchange the blood and captive populations of small size become inbred or extinct.

Population size is without any doubt the most important factor of population viability (Raup 1991, Wilson 1992, Frankham et al. 2002). Small populations are prone to rapid extinction especially due to stochastic demographic factors (Lande 1999) and negative effects of accumulation of deleterious mutations via genetic drift and/or inbreeding (Kimura 1983, Lande 1999, Rodrígez-Clarc1999, Frankham et al. 2002). Both these processes decrease sharply with increasing population size and thus large populations are much safer than the smaller ones. As the theory of population viability is complex and many parameters necessary for its estimates are usually not easily available for particular species, we adopted straightforward arbitrary criteria based solely on the size of the zoo population worldwide. Our approach was based on empirical experience that the minimum population size necessary for short-time captive maintenance of animal species/breed under controlled conditions is about 50 (Soulé 1980), and populations over about 500 individuals are not affected by inbreeding depression (Reed et al. 2007). Nevertheless, we keep in mind that the theory suggests rather continuous increase of the risks as well as its dependence on population history, generation time, and many other parameters (for review see Frankham et al. 2002). Moreover, estimates of minimum viable population are much larger: amphibian and reptiles 5,409, birds 3,742 and mammals 3,876 individuals (Traill et al. 2007).

We focused on the species whose zoo populations exceeded these arbitrary criteria and found 247 (28) reptiles, 634 (80) birds, and 416 (79) mammals with zoo populations over 50 and 500 (given in parentheses) individuals. Although one might perceive these values as small and invaluable, we consider the support of 2.9% (0.3%) of reptile, 6.6% (0.8%) of bird and 7.8% (1.5%) of mammalian species relevant enough to justify funding of the zoos.

Chapter 4

RELATIVE REPRESENTATION OF ENDANGERED SPECIES

Not all vertebrate species are currently at risk of extinction; therefore the beneficial role of captive breeding in conservation of global species diversity may be enhanced by selective keeping of endangered species. We analyze here the representation of the species listed by IUCN in the categories "nearly threatened" or higher. Among the studied vertebrate classes, there are 481 reptiles (5.6% of extant species), 1869 birds (19.4%), and 1145 mammals (21.4%) of these categories (further referred as IUCN species). Thus, reptiles seem to be nearly four times less endangered than birds or mammals. Otherwise, they may be just less frequently listed in IUCN categories as members of the group attracting less human attention.

Zoos keep 167 IUCN species of reptiles, 364 IUCN species of birds and 250 IUCN species of mammals (Table 2). Interestingly enough, the IUCN species are nearly three times more represented among the zoo species of reptiles (34.7%) than among those absent in zoos (12.7%; χ^2=198.7, df=1, P<0.0001). The corresponding difference was much smaller for mammals (25.3 versus 20.6%, χ^2=10.4, df=1, P<0.0012). For birds we found an inverse relationship with the IUCN species being underrepresented in zoos: 15.6 versus 20.6% (χ^2=29.1, df=1, P<0.0001).

Besides the presence or absence of the IUCN species in zoos, there is an even more important issue: the population size of these species supported by the global network of zoos. Fortunately, mean zoo populations of the IUCN species are as a rule somewhat larger than those of less endangered. This difference was higher in reptiles (27.5 versus 11.1 individuals; t-test: t=6.51, df=1152, P<0.0001) than in birds (23.7 versus 13.3; t=5.50, df=2334, P<0.0001) and mammals (48.0 versus 28.4; t=4.07, P=0.0001; see Table 2).

More illustrative are plots comparing distribution of population sizes among the IUCN and non-IUCN species (Fig. 1-3). In addition to overrepresentation of the IUCN taxa, it is clearly visible that within each analyzed class, a handful percent of the species with the largest population sizes in zoos are apparently overrepresented as their data points deviates from the strait line characterizing the remaining species.

Table 2. Representation of endangered species in zoo collections.

Class:	Reptiles	Birds	Mammals
number of living IUCN species (degree of "nearly threatened" or more)	481	1869	1148
number of IUCN species kept in zoos	167	364	250
IUCN species with zoo population size over 50	70	141	130
IUCN species with zoo population size over 500	6	20	23
mean size of zoo population of IUCN species*	11.1	23.7	26.4
number of living non-IUCN species	8121	7758	4205
number of non-IUCN species kept in zoos	988	1973	740
non-IUCN species with zoo population size over 50	177	492	286
non-IUCN species with zoo population size over 500	22	60	56
mean size of zoo population of non-IUCN species*	27.5	13.3	48

*Computed from log transformed data.

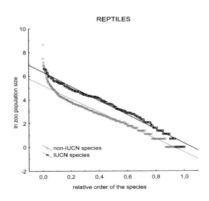

Figure 1. Size distribution of worldwide zoo populations of reptiles: a comparison of endangered species (IUCN category NT-nearly threatened or higher) with the remaining ones (non-IUCN). ln population size = log transformed number of individuals of a given species kept in zoos worldwide. Population sizes are sorted in descending order on the x axis. Order of each species was scaled to the total number of IUCN or non-IUCN species.

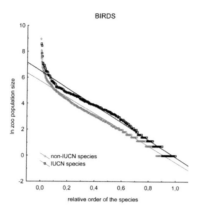

Figure 2. Size distribution of zoo populations of birds: a comparison of endangered species (IUCN category NT-nearly threatened or higher) with the remaining ones (non-IUCN). ln population size = log transformed number of individuals of a given species kept in zoos worldwide. Population sizes are sorted in descending order on the x axis. Order of each species was scaled to the total number of IUCN or non-IUCN species.

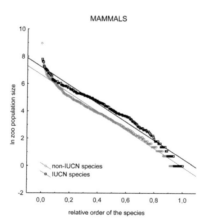

Figure 3. Size distribution of zoo populations of mammals: a comparison of endangered species (IUCN category NT-nearly threatened or higher) with the remaining ones (non-IUCN). ln population size = log transformed number of individuals of a given species kept in zoos worldwide. Population sizes are sorted in descending order on the x axis. Order of each species was scaled to the total number of IUCN or non-IUCN species.

That is why we paid special attention to the species whose zoo populations are large enough to secure short-term survival in captivity.

Chapter 5

EFFECTS OF PERCEIVED ATTRACTIVENESS AND BODY SIZE AMONG RELATED SPECIES

PYTHONS AND BOAS

Recently, we studied human preferences towards a representative sample of 56 species of pythons and boas of the family Boidae. Colorful and patterned species such as the rainbow boa (*Epicrates cenchria cenchria*), ball python (*Python regius*), Burmese python (*Python molurus bivittatus*), red blood python (*P. brongesmai*), Emerald tree boa (*Corallus caninus*) were most preferred, while brownish Hispaniola boa (*Epicrates gracilis*), Puerto Rican boa (*E.inornatus*), olive python (*Liasis olivaceus*), Indian sand boa (*Eryx johni*), ringed tree boa (*Corallus annulatus*) were least preferred. We clearly demonstrated that the sizes of the worldwide zoo populations of individual boid species are closely correlated with both body size and human preferences (β=0.39 and -0.39; Marešová and Frynta 2008). The question was whether such a close dependence of the zoo population on factors reflecting sensory and/or emotional stimulation of the visitors/keepers is universal or is confined to the specific taxa such as snakes evoking arousal in most human beings. To answer this question we also performed similar experiments also in turtles as well as in one bird and one mammalian group.

TURTLES

Captive breeding programs are really fundamental for survival of several species of turtles and tortoises (Testudines) which are heavily exploited or even extinct in the wild. Thus zoos may play an important role in conservation of these animals. Currently, ISIS reports in zoos 31,078 individuals belonging to 221 species (of about 298 extant species of chelonians). Since zoo visitors perceive turtles as a very homogenous group, we had to include the species representing all turtle subfamilies to increase both taxonomic and morphological variation. In this analysis we selected the most abundant zoo species and the subfamilies exceeding 20 extant species that were represented by two most abundant species kept in zoos. There was a fairly good agreement among the 25 respondents; PC1 explained 57% of the total variation in species ranks.

Next, we excluded three obligatory marine species that are difficult to keep in zoos and carried out the GLM analysis. The size of the zoo population was significantly predicted by human aesthetic preferences ($F_{(1,23)}$=6.3, P=0.0197), but not by body size ($F_{(1,23)}$=3.8, P=0.0647) or IUCN listing ($F_{(1,23)}$=1.7, P=0.2081). The correlation between human aesthetic preference and size of zoo populations (Figure 4) was only moderate (r=-0.492), but highly significant (P<0.0107).

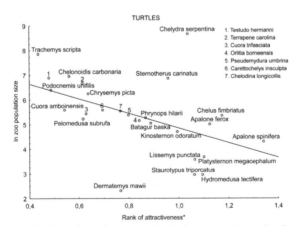

*Please note that the higher value of mean rank, the less attractive animal.

Figure 4. Relationship between size of zoo populations and human preferences in turtles (Testudines). Rank of attractiveness = mean square-root arcsin transformed rank. In zoo population size = log transformed number of individuals of a given species kept in zoos worldwide. R2 = 24.2%, P = 0.0107, y = 7.83 * x -2.97.

The most deviating point from this relationship represents the common snapping turtle (*Chelydra serpentina*). Although the zoo population of this species is the largest, it was not preferred by our respondents. Nevertheless, this discrepancy may be easily explained by emotional arousal induced by the dangerous species.

PHEASANTS

Pheasants and allies of the family Phasianidae (sensu del Hoyo 1992-2002, i.e., excluding Tetraonidae and Meleagridae) are frequently kept and bred in zoos; in total 9,731 individuals belonging to 79 species are reported by ISIS. We sorted these species according to size of zoo populations, and selected every even one for further analysis. Next we tested human aesthetic preferences towards these 40 species and found a good agreement among respondents; the first principal component explained 35.2% of the total variation. Species exhibiting elaborated tail feathers and/or loud colours such as Indian peafowl (*Pavo cristatus*), Lady Amherst's pheasant (*Chrysolophus amherstiae*), Reeve's pheasant (*Syrmaticus reevesii*), silver pheasant (*Lophura nycthemera*), Swinhoe's pheasant (*Lophura swinhoii*) were most preferred while short-tailed dull ones such as Cabot's tragopan (*Tragopan caboti*), Salwadori's pheasant (*Lophura inornata*), brown quail (*Coturnix ypsilophora*), Hildebrandt's francolin (*Francolinus hildebrandti*), Natal francolin (*F. natalensis*) were least preferred.

The GLM analysis revealed the human aesthetic preference ($F_{(1,36)}$=16.6, P=0.0002), but not body size ($F_{(1,36)}$=2.6, P=0.1119) or IUCN listing ($F_{(1,36)}$=0.02, P=0.8882), to be a relevant predictor of the zoo population size. The correlation between human aesthetic preference and size of zoo populations was high enough (r=-0.601; P<0.0001) to be worth of conservationists' attention (Figure 5).

ANTELOPES AND ALLIES

The family Bovidae comprising 138 extant species of antelopes, goats, sheep and buffaloes belong to the hard core of the zoo animals. ISIS recorded 26,794 individuals in zoos belonging to 96 species. Similarly as in the case of pheasants we sorted the species according to the zoo population size and selected a set of 45 species (every even one represented in zoos by more than 12 individuals) for further analysis. The first principal component explained only 26% of the total variance, thus the agreement among the respondents was poorer than in the case of pheasants. Consequently, the GLM analyses revealed that size of zoo populations can be explained neither by human aesthetic preferences ($F_{(1,44)}=0.31$, $P=0.5793$) nor by IUCN listing ($F_{(1,44)}=1.87$, $P=0.1782$). Body size has remained the only significant predictor of the zoo population size ($F_{(1,44)}=5.23$, $P=0.0270$, Figure 6).

Although antelopes and allies vary in their body form and/or in the presence and shape of their horns (Caro et al. 2003), their coloration is rather uniform as in most mammalian taxa. Therefore, body size is the only other stimulus that may influence decision making of zoo visitors and keepers.

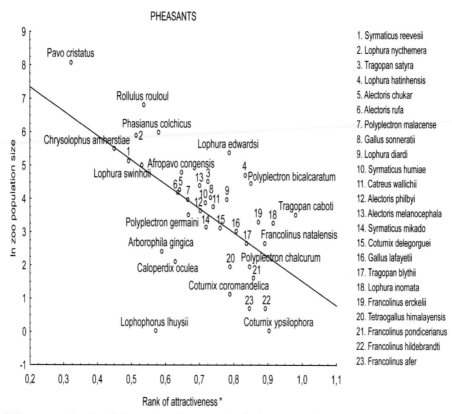

*Please note that the higher value of mean rank, the less attractive animal.

Figure 5. Relationship between size of zoo populations and human preferences in pheasants (Phasianidae). Rank of attractiveness = mean square-root arcsin transformed rank. ln zoo population size = log transformed number of individuals of a given species kept in zoos worldwide. $R2 = 36.1\%$, $P < 0.0001$, $y = -8.81 * x -7.29$.

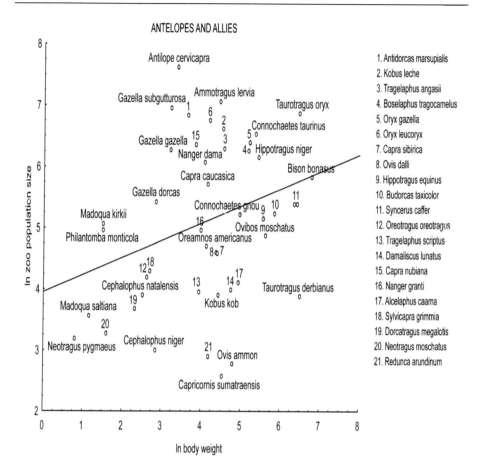

Figure 6. Relationship between size of zoo populations and body size in antelopes and allies (Bovidae). ln zoo population size = log transformed number of individuals of a given species kept in zoos worldwide. $R^2 = 10.3\%$, $P = 0.0261$, $y = 3.91 * x + 0.29$.

Chapter 6

EFFECTS OF PERCEIVED ATTRACTIVENESS AND BODY SIZE ON HIGHER TAXONOMIC SCALE

The results provided in the previous paragraphs suggest that aesthetic preferences towards particular species are correlated with zoo population size in several vertebrate taxa. Nevertheless, not only the extinction of individual species, but also the extinction of higher taxa poses a major threat to global biodiversity. Therefore, we also carried out similar analyses for presumably monophyletic groups on the family and/or subfamily scale.

For this purpose we split the studied classes of vertebrates into eleven more homogenous groups, each consisting of two or three dozens of families/ subfamilies or other monophyletic taxa of comparable level (or more detailed in the case of primates, in accord with Goodman et al.1998). Reptiles were split into three morphologically (for recent phylogenies see Towsend et al 2004, Vidal and Hedges 2005, Uetz et al. 2008) distinct groups: snakes (Ophidia), lizards (tuataras and squamates except snakes) and turtles (Testudines). Birds are a morphologically most homogenous class of terrestrial vertebrates. Moreover, phylogeny (Sibley and Ahlquist 1990, Ericson et al. 2006, Hackett et al. 2008) does not reflect the variability in appearance properly. We analyzed the following groups defined by a combination of the phylogenetic (Ericson et al. 2006) and ecomorphological features: "basal birds" (Paleognathae, Galloanserae and Columbidae belonging to Metaves), "aquatic birds" (belonging to Neoaves and Metaves), "terrestrial birds" (selected Neoaves) and "passerines" (Passeriformes: Passerida; Barker et al. 2004). Mammals were split based on the purely phylogenetic criteria (Murphy et al. 2001, Bininda-Emonds 2007) into following four groups: "basal mammals" (Monotremata, Metatheria, Xenarthra, Afrotheria), "Glires" (Rodentia and Lagomorpha), "Euarchonta" (Scandentia, Dermoptera and Primates), and finally "Laurasiatheria" (Eulipotyphla, Artiodactyla, Perissodactyla, Pholidota and Carnivora; Cetacea and Chiroptera were omitted because of their specific requirements and deviation of typical mammalian life style).

Each of these families/subfamilies was characterized by the total number of individuals kept in zoos worldwide, the number of extant species, the typical body size (i.e., weight for birds and mammals, and length for reptiles) and estimated of human preference. To assess the last variable we randomly selected one (or more) species of each family/subfamily from the complete species list and included them into the set of pictures presented to our respondents (for more details see Data sources and testing procedures). When no relevant picture was available for the particular species, we repeated random selection once again. When pictures of more than one species belonging to the group were included in the test, the data were pooled to avoid pseudoreplication.

Multiple regression, in which log-transformed number of individuals per species (i.e., mean population size) was given as a dependent variable, and log-transformed body size and human preference as independent (explanatory) variables, was computed for each studied vertebrate group. All these eleven models computed for particular vertebrate groups except one (turtles) were significant and explained enough variation to be considered in conservation biology (see Table 3).

In accord with expectations, body size was the best predictor of the number of individuals per species. Its effect was positive in ten out of eleven analyzed groups (except turtles); nine of these effects were significant ($P<0.05$) and one (group of "basal mammals") approached significance ($P<0.1$). The larger the typical species of the family/subfamily is, the more individuals per species are kept in zoos. This relationship was really strong within most studied groups, in particular snakes and Laurasiatheria (Figures 7-8, 10-12, 14, 16-18). The only exception were turtles exhibiting even an inverse relationship, which was, however, statistically insignificant.

Human preference contributed less apparently to the models explaining the number of individuals per species. Interestingly enough, the effects of ranking were always negative, i.e., the higher the human preference, the better the representation of the given family/subfamily in zoos. However, this factor reached formal statistical significance ($P<0.05$) only in two mamamlian ("basal mammals" and Laurasiatheria) and one bird ("terrestrial birds") groups (see Figures 15, 13).

Table 3. Results of multiple regression explaining zoo population per species (log-transformed) by body size (log-transformed) and human preferences (square root arcsin transformed ranks).

Higher taxonomic groups	Body size - median for particular family/subfamily			Rank of perceived attractiveness			Explained variance by PC1	number of respondents	Summary of regression model
	β	t	p <	β	t	p <	PC1	N	
Reptiles									
Snakes	0.721	5.76	0.0001	-0.024	-0.19	0.8497	48.0%	32	$R2=0.5289$; $F_{(2.32)}=18.0$; $p<.0001$
Lepidosauria except snakes	0.536	3.85	0.0001	-0.203	-1.46	0.1548	38.5%	50	$R2=0.3429$; $F_{(2.34)}=8.9$; $p<.0008$
Turtles	-0.214	-1.00	0.3319	-0.389	-1.81	0.0868	47.5%	53	$R2=0.1788$; $F_{(2.18)}=2.0$; $p<.1697$
Birds									
Basal birds	0.638	4.20	0.0003	-0.273	-1.80	0.0826	24.1%	36	$R2=0.3939$; $F_{(2.28)}=9.1$; $p<.0009$
Aquatic birds	0.463	2.86	0.0084	-0.306	-1.89	0.0704	31.6%	36	$R2=0.4144$; $F_{(2.26)}=9.2$; $p<.0010$
Terrestrial birds	0.541	3.22	0.0039	-0.353	-2.10	0.0473	32.4%	36	$R2=0.3277$; $F_{(2.22)}=6.8$; $p<.0049$
Passerines	0.525	3.20	0.0035	-0.284	-1.74	0.0940	17.2%	36	$R2=0.3006$; $F_{(2.27)}=5.8$; $p<.0080$

Table 3. (Continued).

Higher taxonomic groups	Body size - median for particular family/subfamily			Rank of perceived attractiveness			Explained variance by PC1	number of respondents	Summary of regression model
	β	t	p <	β	t	p <	PC1	N	
Mammals									
Bassal mammals	0.260	1.70	0.0986	-0.417	-2.73	0.0102	28.3%	45	$R2=0.2885; F_{(2,32)}=6.5; p<.0043$
Glires	0.397	2.38	0.0238	-0.242	-1.45	0.1577	42.4%	52	$R2=0.1863; F_{(2,30)}=3.4; p<.0454$
Euarchonta	0.482	2.71	0.0110	-0.150	-0.84	0.4055	21.5%	51	$R2=0.1979; F_{(2,30)}=3.7; p<.0366$
Laurasiatheria	0.663348	5.29177	0.000010	-0.277793	-2.21605	0.034418	20.4%	42	$R2=0.5291; F_{(2,30)}=16.9; p<.0001$

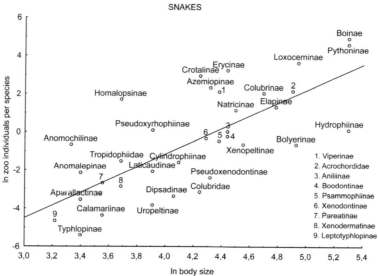

Specimen species representing the taxa sorted according to rank of attractiveness in descending order: Parias flavomaculatus (Crotalinae), Geophis semidoliatus (Dipsadinae), Anilius scytale (Aniliinae), Laticauda colubrina (Laticaudinae), Cercaspis carinata (Colubridae incertae sedis), Atractaspis bibronii (Aparallactinae, Atractaspidinae), Xenopeltis unicolor (Xenopeltinae), Azemiops feae (Azemiopinae), Acrantophis madagascariensis (Boinae), Hydrophis cyanocinctus (Hydrophiinae), Cylindrophis maculatus (Cylindrophiinae), Tropidophis greenwayi (Tropidophiidae, Ungaliophiidae), Vipera ursinii (Viperinae), Acrochordus granulatus (Acrochordidae), Pseudoxenodon macrops (Pseudoxenodontinae), Boulengerina annulata stormsi (Elapinae), Enhydris enhydris (Homalopsinae), Achalinus spinalis (Xenodermatinae), Ialtris dorsalis (Xenodontinae), Anomochilus weberi (Anomochilinae), Pareas monticola (Pareatinae), Psammophis schokari (Psammophiinae), Calmaria schmidti (Calamariinae), Amphiesma platyceps (Natricinae), Antaresia maculosa (Pythoninae), Ithycyphus miniatus (Pseudoxyrhophiinae), Eryx colubrinus (Erycinae), Lycodomorphus bicolor (Boodontinae), Loxocemus bicolor (Loxoceminae), Tantilla coronata (Colubrinae), Rhinophis pillippinus (Uropeltinae), Casarea dussumieri (Bolyerinae), Leptotyphlops humilis (Leptotyphlopinae), Liotyphlops beui (Anomalepinae), Typhlops brongersmianus (Typhlopinae).

Figure 7. Relationship between size of zoo populations per species and body size in snakes. Ln zoo individuals per species = log-transformed number of individuals belonging to a given family/subfamily kept in zoos worldwide per the total number of living species in this group. ln body size = log-transformed length. $R^2 = 52.8\%$; $P < 0.0001$, $y = -14.53 * x + 3.35$.

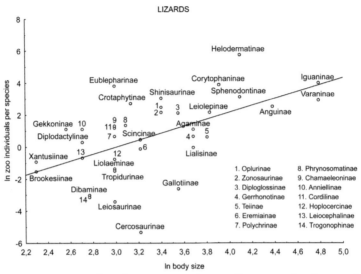

Specimen species representing the taxa sorted according to rank of attractiveness in descending order: Chamaeleo rudis (Chamaeleoninae), Oplurus fierinensis (Oplurinae), Microlophus thoracicus (Tropidurinae), Abronia vasconcelosii (Gerrhonotinae), Cnemidophorus gularis (Teiinae), Heloderma suspectum (Helodermatinae), Leiocephalus l. lunatus (Leiocephalinae), Lepidophyma sylvaticum (Xantusiinae), Liolaemus chiliensis (Liolaeminae), Heliobolus spekii (Eremiainae), Ctenophorus fordi (Agaminae), Eublepharis hardwickii (Eublepharinae), Cordylus tropidosternum (Cordilinae), Varanus niloticus (Varaninae), Zonosaurus quadrilineatus (Zonosaurinae), Heteronotia binolei (Gekkoninae), Crotaphytus antiquus (Crotaphytinae), Pristidactylus torquatus (Leiosaurinae), Anolis wattsi (Polychrinae), Corytophanes hernandesii (Corytophaninae), Schinisaurus crocodylurus (Shinisaurinae), Galotia galloti (Galotiinae), Hoplocercus spinosus (Hoplocercinae), Dipsosaurus dorsalis (Iguaninae), Sphenodon punctatus (Sphenodontinae), Saltuarius cornutus (Diplodactylinae), Potamites apodemus (Cercosaurinae), Lankascincus deraniyagalai (Scincinae), Celestus stenurus (Diploglossinae), Sceloporus spinosus (Phrynosomatinae), Rhampholeon boulengeri (Brookesiinae), Ophisaurus atennuatus (Anguinae), Uromastyx aegyptia (Leiolepinae or Leiolepidinae), Trogonophis wiegmani (Trogonophinae), Aprasia rostrata (Lialisinae or Pygopodinae), Dibamus bogadeki (Dibaminae), Anniella pulchra (Anniellinae).

Figure 8. Relationship between size of zoo populations per species and body size in lizards (including tuataras). ln zoo individuals per species = log-transformed number of individuals belonging to a given family/subfamily kept in zoos worldwide per the total number of living species in this group. ln body size = log-transformed snout-vent length. R = 30.5%, P= 0.0004, y = -6,52 * x +2,17.

In additional one reptile (turtles; Figure 9) and three bird groups ("basal birds", "aquatic birds" and "passerines") this factor approached significance (P<0.1).

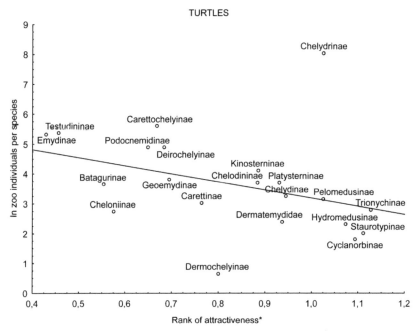

*Please note that the higher value of mean rank, the less attractive animal.

Specimen species representing the taxa sorted according to rank of attractiveness in descending order: Clemmys guttata (Emydinae), Astrochelys yniphora (Testudininae), Malayemys subrijuga (Batagurinae), Chelonia mydas (Cheloniinae), Podocnemis erythrocephala (Podocnemidinae), Carettochelys insculpta (Caretochelynae), Pseudemys nelsoni (Deirochelyinae), Cuora trifasciata (Geoemydinae), Lepidochelys olivacea (Carettinae), Dermochelys coriacea (Dermochelyinae), Elseya albagula (Chelodininae), Kinosternon flavescens (Kinosterninae), Platysternon megacephalum (Platysterninae), Dermatemys mawii (Dermatemydidae), Phrynops hilari (Chelidinae), Chelydra serpentina (Chelydrinae), Pelusios castanoides (Pelomedusinae), Hydromedusa tectifera (Hydromedusinae), Lissemys punctata (Cyclanorbinae), Staurotypus triporcatus (Staurotypinae), Apalone ferox (Trionychinae).

Figure 9. Relationship between size of zoo populations per species and attractiveness in turtles. ln zoo individuals per species = log-transformed number of individuals belonging to a given family/subfamily kept in zoos worldwide per the total number of living species in this group. Rank of attractiveness = mean square-root arcsin transformed rank. R2 = 13.35%, P = 0.1034, y = 59.0 * x -2.71.

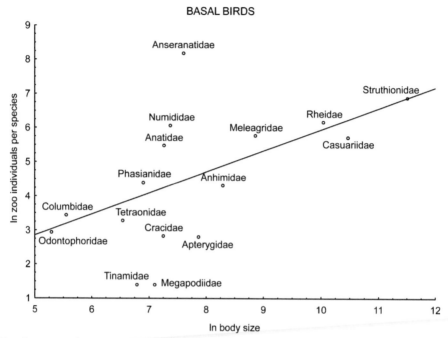

Specimen species representing the taxa sorted according to rank of attractiveness in descending order: Apteryx australis (Apterygidae); Chalcophaps stephani, Ptilinopus arcanus, Treron oxyura, Geophaps scripta, Columba delegorguei, Zenaida aurita (Columbidae), Bonasa bonasia (Tetraonidae); Chloephaga poliocephala, Anas undulata, Oxyura maccoa, Tadorna radjah (Anatidae); Rhea pennata (Rheidae); Struthio camelus (Struthionidae); Callipepla squamata, Odontophorus hyperythrus (Odontophoridae); Margaroperdix madagarensis, Tetraogallus caucasicus, Argusianus argus, Gallus sonneratii, Francolinus rufopictus (Phasianidae); Chauna chavaria (Anhimidae); Casuarius casuarius (Casuariidae); Guttera plumifera (Numididae); Ortalis erythroptera, Penelope ortoni (Cracidae); Anseranas semipalmata (Anseranatidae); Nothocercus julius, Tinamus tao (Tinamidae); Meleagris gallopavo (Meleagridae); Megapodius laperouse (Megapodiidae).

Figure 10. Relationship between size of zoo populations per species and body size in basal birds. ln zoo individuals per species = log-transformed number of individuals belonging to a given family/subfamily kept in zoos worldwide per the total number of living species in this group. ln body size = log-transformed weight. $R2 = 32.4\%$, $P = 0.0008$; $y = -0.24 * x + 0.62$.

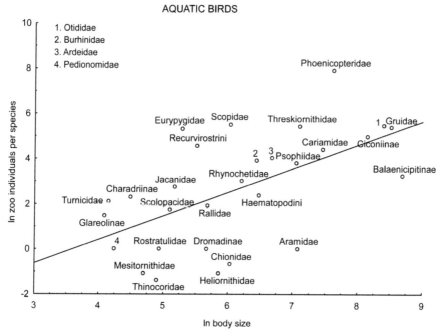

Specimen species representing the taxa sorted according to rank of attractiveness in descending order: Phoenicopterus ruber (Phoenicopteridae), Balearica pavonina (Gruidae), Himantopus mexicanus (Recurvirostrini), Aramus guarauna (Aramidae), Ardea humbloti (Ardeidae), Ciconia nigra (Ciconiinae), Dromas ardeola (Dromadinae), Jacana jacana (Jacanidae), Eupodotis caerulescens (Otididae), Eurypyga helias (Eurypygidae), Theristicus melanopis (Threskiornithidae), Balaeniceps rex (Balaenicipitinae), Vanellus melanocephalus (Charadriinae), Rostratula semicollaris (Rostratulidae), Scopus umbretta (Scopidae), Glareola ocularis (Glareolinae), Tringa incana (Scolopacidae), Psophia leucoptera (Psophiidae), Heliopais personata (Heliornithidae), Pedionomus torquatus (Pedionomidae), Burhinus recurvirostris (Burhinidae), Haematopus moquini (Haematopodini), Monias benschi (Mesitornithidae), Thinocorus orbignyianus (Thinocoridae), Amaurolimnas concolor (Rallidae), Rhynochetos jubatus (Rhynochetidae), Turnix velox (Turnicidae), Chunga burmeisteri (Cariamidae), Chionis alba (Chionidae).

Figure 11. Relationship between size of zoo populations per species and body size in aquatic birds. ln zoo individuals per species = log-transformed number of individuals belonging to a given family/subfamily kept in zoos worldwide per the total number of living species in this group. ln body size = log-transformed weight. $R2 = 33.4\%$, $P = 0.0010$, $y = -3.76 * x + 1.05$.

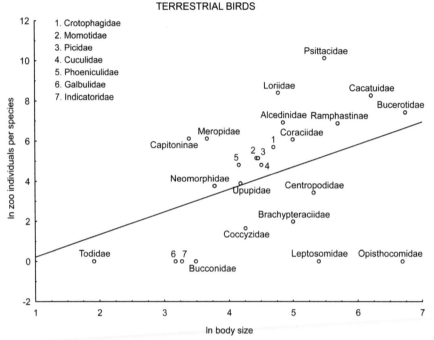

Specimen species representing the taxa sorted according to rank of attractiveness in descending order: Alcedo cyanopecta, Halcyon smyrnensis, Megaceryle alcyon (Alcedinidae); Momotus mexicanus (Momotidae); Upupa epops (Upupidae); Merops boehmi (Meropidae); Aulacorhynchus prasinus (Ramphastinae); Ara chloropterus, Bolborhynchus ferrugineifrons (Psittacidae); Jacamerops aureus (Galbulidae); Todus multicolor (Todidae); Charmosyna rubronotata (Loriidae); Phoeniculus staneiceps (Phoeniculidae); Coracias naevia (Coraciidae); Opisthocomus hoazin (Opisthocomidae); Dryocopus pileatus, Picumnus pygmaeus (Picidae); Uratelornis chimaera (Brachypteraciidae); Cacatua alba (Cacatuidae); Tricholaema frontata, Semnornis ramphastinus (Capitoninae); Anorrhinus galeritus (Bucerotidae); Leptosomus discolor (Leptosomidae); Neomorphus geoffroyi (Neomorphidae); Coccyzus lansbergi (Coccyzidae); Eudynamys scolopacea (Cuculidae); Malacoptila rufa (Bucconidae); Centropus violaceus (Centropodidae); Crotophaga sulcirostris (Crotophagidae); Indicator willcocksi (Indicatoridae).

Figure 12. Relationship between size of zoo populations per species and body size in terrestrial birds. ln zoo individuals per species = log-transformed number of individuals belonging to a given family/subfamily kept in zoos worldwide per the total number of living species in this group. ln body size = log-transformed weight. R2 = 17.1%; P = 0.0399, y = -0,89 * x + 1,12.

Effects of Perceived Attractiveness and Body Size on Higher ...

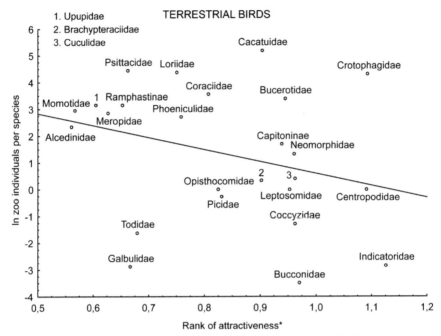

*Please note that the higher value of mean rank, the less attractive animal.

Specimen species representing the taxa sorted according to rank of attractiveness in descending order: Alcedo cyanopecta, Halcyon smyrnensis, Megaceryle alcyon (Alcedinidae); Momotus mexicanus (Momotidae); Upupa epops (Upupidae); Merops boehmi (Meropidae); Aulacorhynchus prasinus (Ramphastinae); Ara chloropterus, Bolborhynchus ferrugineifrons (Psittacidae); Jacamerops aureus (Galbulidae); Todus multicolor (Todidae); Charmosyna rubronotata (Loriidae); Phoeniculus staneiceps (Phoeniculidae); Coracias naevia (Coraciidae); Opisthocomus hoazin (Opisthocomidae); Dryocopus pileatus, Picumnus pygmaeus (Picidae); Uratelornis chimaera (Brachypteraciidae); Cacatua alba (Cacatuidae); Tricholaema frontata, Semnornis ramphastinus (Capitoninae); Anorrhinus galeritus (Bucerotidae); Leptosomus discolor (Leptosomidae); Neomorphus geoffroyi (Neomorphidae); Coccyzus lansbergi (Coccyzidae); Eudynamys scolopacea (Cuculidae); Malacoptila rufa (Bucconidae); Centropus violaceus (Centropodidae); Crotophaga sulcirostris (Crotophagidae); Indicator willcocksi (Indicatoridae).

Figure 13. Relationship between size of zoo populations per species and attractiveness in terrestrial birds. ln zoo individuals per species = log-transformed number of individuals belonging to a given family/subfamily kept in zoos worldwide per the total number of living species in this group. Rank of attractiveness = mean square-root arcsin transformed rank. $R^2 = 09.3\%$, $P = 0.14$, $y = 5.07 * x - 4.47$.

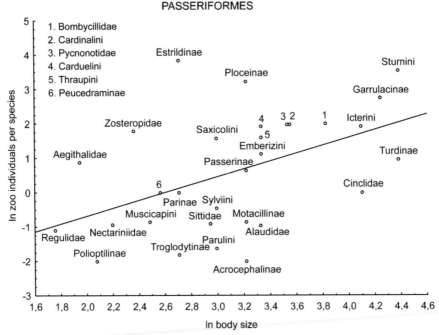

Specimen species representing the taxa sorted according to rank of attractiveness in descending order: Cyanoptila cyanomelaena (Muscicapini), Parus caeruleus (Parinae), Peucedramus taeniatus (Peucedraminae), Parula americana (Parulini), Aethopyga siparaja (Nectariniidae), Passerina ciris (Cardinalini), Uraeginthus angolensis (Estrildinae), Ploceus cucullatus (Ploceinae), Regulus teneriffae (Regulidae), Pycnonotus jocosus (Pycnonotidae), Passer Melanurus (Passerinae), Garrulax pectoralis (Garrulacinae), Phoenicurus auroreus (Saxicolini), Loxia curvirostra (Carduelini), Gracula religiosa (Sturnini), Bombycilla cedrorum (Bombycillidae), Sitta europaea (Sittidae), Zosterops palpebrosus (Zosteropidae), Emberiza citrinella (Emberizini), Bradypterus seebohmi (Acrocephalinae), Cinclus cinclus (Cinclidae), Thryothorus ludovicianus (Troglodytinae), Polioptila caerulea (Polioptilinae), Molothrus ater (Icterini), Catharus guttatus (Turdinae), Anthus campestris (Motacillinae), Sylvia melanocephala (Sylviini) Mirafra erythroptera (Alaudidae), Aegithalos caudatus (Aegithalidae), Coereba flaveola (Thraupini).

Figure 14. Relationship between size of zoo populations per species and body size in passerines. In zoo individuals per species = log-transformed number of individuals belonging to a given family/subfamily kept in zoos worldwide per the total number of living species in this group. In body size = log-transformed weight. R^2 = 22.3%, P = 0.0085, y = -2.96 * x + 1,14.

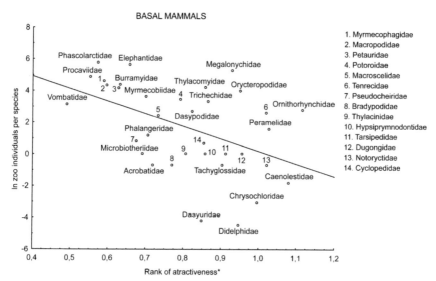

*Please note that the higher value of mean rank, the less attractive animal.

Specimen species representing the taxa sorted according to rank of attractiveness in descending order: Vombatus ursinus (Vombatidae), Dendrohyrax arboreus (Procaviidae), Phascolarctos cinereus (Phascolarctidae), Tamandua mexicana (Myrmecophagidae), Petrogale xanthopus (Macropodidae), Petaurus norfolcensis (Petauridae), Cercartetus nanus (Burramyidae), Loxodonta africana (Elephantidae), Pseudocheirus peregrinus (Pseudocheiridae), Dromiciops gliroides (Microbiotheriidae), Myrmecobius fasciatus (Myrmecobiidae), Trichosurus caninus (Phalangeridae), Distoechurus pennatus (Acrobatidae), Macroscelides proboscideus (Macroscelidae), Bradypus tridactylus (Bradypodidae), Aepyprymnus rufescens (Potoroidae), Thylacinus cynocephalus (Thylacinidae), Chaetophractus vellerosus (Dasypodidae), Sminthopsis murina (Dasyuridae), Cyclopes didactylus (Cyclopedidae), Hypsiprymnodon moschatus (Hypsiprymnodontidae), Macrotis lagotis (Thylacomyidae), Trichechus manatus (Trichechidae), Zaglossus bruijni (Tachyglossidae), Tarsipes rostratus (Tarsipedidae) Choloepus didactylus (Megalonychidae), Marmosa murina (Didelphidae), Orycteropus afer (Orycteropodidae), Dugong dugon (Dugongidae), Cryptochloris asiatica (Chrysochloridae), Microgale taiva (Tenrecidae), Notoryctes caurinus (Notoryctidae), Perameles gunnii, (Peramelidae), Lestoros inca (Caenolestidae), Ornithorhynchus anatinus (Ornithorhynchidae).

Figure 15. Relationship between size of zoo populations per species and attractiveness in basal mammals including Prototheria, Methatheria, Xenarthra and Afrotheria. In zoo individuals per species = log-transformed number of individuals belonging to a given family/subfamily kept in zoos worldwide per the total number of living species in this group. Rank of attractiveness = mean square-root arcsin transformed rank. R2 = 22.4%, P = 0.0041, y = 8.09 * x − 7.92.

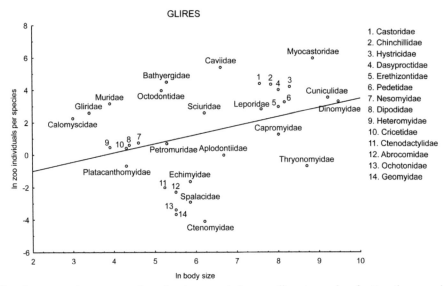

Specimen species representing the taxa sorted according to rank of attractiveness in descending order: Ochotona alpina (Ochotonidae), Petromus typicus (Petromuridae), Octodon degu (Octodontidae), Macrotarsomys bastardi (Nesomyidae), Graphiurus kelleni (Gliridae), Sylvilagus obscurus (Leporidae), Dolichotis patagonum (Caviidae), Spermophilus columbianus (Sciuridae), Chaetodipus baileyi (Heteromyidae), Pedetes capensis (Pedetidae), Dasyprocta leporina (Dasyproctidae), Calomyscus (Calomyscidae), Dinomys branickii (Dinomyidae), Platacanthomys lasiurus (Platacanthomyidae), Allactaga elater (Dipodidae), Massoutiera mzabi (Echimyidae), Lagostomus maximus (Chinchillidae), Cuniculus paca (Cuniculidae), Apodemus agrarius (Muridae), Atherurus africanus (Hystricidae), Castor canadensis (Castoridae), Capromys pilorides (Capromyidae), Proechimys guarirae (Ctenodactylidae), Myocastor coypus (Myocastoridae), Ctenomys (Ctenomyidae), Thryonomys swinderianus (Thryonomyidae), Geomys (Geomyidae), Aplodontia rufa (Aplodontiidae), Melanomys caliginosus (Cricetidae), Abrocoma benettii (Abrocomidae), Cryptomys mechowi (Bathyergidae), Coendou prehensilis (Erethizontidae), Spalax leucodon (Spalacidae).

Figure 16. Relationship between size of zoo populations per species and body size in Glires. ln zoo individuals per species = log-transformed number of individuals belonging to a given family/subfamily kept in zoos worldwide per the total number of living species in this group. ln body size = log-transformed weight. $R2 = 12.9\%$, $P = 0.0398$, $y = -2.12 * x + 0.56$.

Effects of Perceived Attractiveness and Body Size on Higher ...

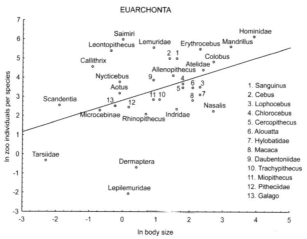

Specimen species representing the taxa sorted according to rank of attractiveness in descending order: Galago rondoensis (Galagidae: Galago, Euoticus, Otolemur); Microcebus ravelobensis (Microcebinae); Lemur catta (Lemuridae); Nycticebus coucang (Lorisidae: Arctocebus, Loris, Perodicticus, Nycticebus, Pseudopotto); Propithecus edwardsi (Indridae); Leontopithecus rosalia (Leontopithecina: Leontopithecus); Miopithecus talapoin (Cercopithecina II: Miopithecus); Callicebus torquatus (Pitheciidae); Cebus olivaceus (Cebinae: Cebus); Saguinus oedipus (Sanguina: Sanguinus, Callimico); Macaca sylvanus (Macaca); Trachypithecus francoisi (Colobinae: Semnopithecus, Trachypithecus, Presbytis); Pongo abelii (Hominidae); Aotus trivirgatus (Aotidae: Aotus); Alouatta caraya (Atelidae: Alouatta); Tarsius syrichta (Tarsiidae); Nomascus concolor (Hylobatidae); Lepilemur septentrionalis (Lepilemuridae); Saimiri oerstedii (Saimirinae: Saimiri); Lophocebus albigena (Lophocebus, Cercocebus); Callithrix pygmaea (Callithrichina: Callithrix); Daubentonia madagascariensis (Daubentoniidae); Mandrillus leucophaeus (Mandrillus, Papio, Theropithecus); Colobus guereza (Colobina: Colobus, Procolobus); Galeopterus variegates (Cynocephalidae: Dermaptera); Cercopithecus diana (Cercopithecina V: Cercopithecus); Chlorocebus aethiops (Cercopithecina IV: Chlorocebus); Allenopithecus nigrovirridis (Cercopithecina I: Allenopithecus); Brachyteles arachnoides (Atelidae: Atelidae except Alouatta); Erythrocebus patas (Cercopithecina III: Erythrocebus); Ptilocercus lowii (Ptilocercidae: Scandentia); Nasalis larvatus (odd-nosed II: Nasalis, Simias) Rhinopithecus roxellana; (odd-nosed I: Rhinopithecus).

Figure 17. Relationship between size of zoo populations per species and body size in Euarchonta. ln zoo individuals per species = log-transformed number of individuals belonging to a given family/subfamily kept in zoos worldwide per the total number of living species in this group. ln body size = log-transformed weight. $R^2 = 17.9\%$, $P = 0.0142$, $y = 2.81 * x + 0.55$.

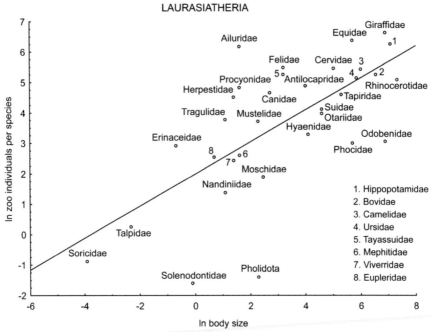

Specimen species representing the taxa sorted according to rank of attractiveness in descending order: Ailurus fulgens (Ailuridae), Hemiechinus auritus (Erinaceidae), Ursus arctos (Ursidae), Leopardus pardalis (Felidae), Giraffa camelopardalis (Giraffidae), Vicugna vicugna (Camelidae), Galidictis fasciata (Eupleridae), Manis culionensis (Pholidota), Crocuta crocuta (Hyaenidae), Moschus moschiferus (Moschidae), Erignathus barbatus (Phocidae), Conepatus semistriatus (Mephitidae), Tragulus javanicus (Tragulidae), Rangifer tarandus (Cervidae), Nasua narica (Procyonidae), Hexaprotodon liberiensis (Hippopotamidae), Diceros bicornis (Rhinocerotidae), Equus grevyi (Equidae), Nyctereutes procyonoides (Canidae), Tayassu pecari (Tayassuidae), Arctocephalus gazella (Otariidae), Genetta genetta (Viverridae), Mungos mungo (Herpestidae), Antilocapra americana (Antilocapridae), Nandinia binotata (Nandiniidae), Sorex minutus (Soricidae), Mellivora capensis (Mustelidae), Odobenus rosmarus (Odobenidae), Talpa europaea (Talpidae), Tapirus bairdii (Tapiridae), Phacochoerus africanus (Suidae), Bos sauveli (Bovidae), Solenodon cubanus (Solenodontidae).

Figure 18. Relationship between size of zoo populations per species and body size in Laurasiatheria. ln zoo individuals per species = log-transformed number of individuals belonging to a given family/subfamily kept in zoos worldwide per the total number of living species in this group. ln body size = log-transformed weight. $R^2 = 45.2\%$, $P = 0.00002$ $y = 1.99 * x + 0.53$.

In conclusion, the relationship between human preference and mean size of zoo population was less apparent, but still detectable, when the analyzed units were the families/subfamilies instead of individual species. Obviously, when comparing families/subfamilies several additional differences in their biological features may mask the relationship. Moreover, decreased strength of the relationship may also be attributed to the fact that not all families/subfamilies are homogenous enough to be reliably represented by a picture of the randomly selected species. This is an especially important factor in the case of morphologically highly homogenous groups (e.g. passerines) in which human preferences are highly determined by coloration, i.e., the character sometimes exhibiting considerable variation even among related species as well as parallel evolution of the same patterns (Chiari et al. 2004). The analysis of 54 published datasets carried out by Areekul and Quicke 2006 confirmed that most color characters (except aposematic or mimetic ones) do not provide good phylogenetic signal and suffer from frequent homoplasies.

Chapter 7

PREFERRED SPECIES AND CHARACTERS

The assessment of human preferences among representatives of families or subfamilies provided us also with additional information.

First, the agreement between the respondents was surprisingly higher for the animal groups least known by the respondent and/or inducing in humans negative rather than positive emotions. The first principal component explained the highest proportion of total variation in such groups as snakes (48.0%), turtles (47.5%), Glires (= rodents and lagomorphs; 42.4%) and lizards (38.5%) are. On the other hand, the lowest agreement among the respondents was recorded in such popular groups as passerines (17.2%), Laurasiatheria (=ungulates, carnivors, pangolins and insectivores; 20.4%) and Euarchonta (primates and allies; 21.5%). Possibly, knowledge or positive attitude towards the animal species may obscure the relationship; while the pictures of unknown animals are ranked solely according to aesthetic rules which are more or less universal (see above).

It is worth of interest, which animals within each particular analyzed group of vertebrates were preferred by our respondents. Top ranking species of each group are listed at the Table 4 and some of them depicted in Figures 19-24. To figure out what taxa/species are perceived by humans as beautiful, indifferent or disgusting, we aligned the set of the pictures according the human's mean ranking in ascending order and tried to interpret the features linked with current position of the picture in whole sequence. Supplementary information was extracted also from remarks of our respondents during the testing.

Table 4. Top ranking species according to human preferences.

Group	The most attractive species	Species perceived as ugly
Snakes	1. Philippine pitviper *Parias flavomaculatus* (Crotalinae) 2. Coral Earth Snake *Geophis semidoliatus* (Dipsadinae) 3. Coral Cylinder Snakes *Anilius scytale* (Aniliinae)	35. Brongersma's Worm Snake *Typhlops brongersmianus* (Typhlopinae) 34. Beu's Dawn Blind Snake *Liotyphlops beui* (Anomalepinae) 33. Western Threadsnake *Leptotyphlops humilis* (Leptotyphlopinae)
Lizards	1. Coarse Chameleon *Chamaeleo rudis* (Chamaeleoninae) 2. Anzamala Madagascar Swift *Oplurus fierinensis* (Oplurinae) 3. Tschudi's Pacific Iguana *Microlophus thoracicus* (Tropidurinae)	37. California legless lizard *Anniella pulchra* (Anniellinae) 36. Blind Lizard *Dibamus bogadeki* (Dibaminae) 35. Exmouth Worm-lizard *Aprasia rostrata* (Lialisinae or Pygopodinae)
Turtles	1. Spotted Turtle *Clemmys guttata* (Emydinae) 2. Madagascan Tortoise *Astrochelys yniphora* (Testudininae) 3. Snail-eating Turtle *Malayemys subtrijuga* (Batagurinae)	21. Florida Softshell Turtle *Apalone ferox* (Trionychinae) 20. Mexican Giant Musk Turtle *Staurotypus triporcatus* (Staurotypinae) 19. Indian Soft-shelled Turtle *Lissemys punctata* (Cyclanorbinae)
Basal birds	1.Brown Kiwi *Apteryx australis* (Apterigidae) 2. Stephan's Dove *Chalcophaps stephani* (Columbidae) 3. Hazel Grouse *Bonasa bonasia* (Tetraonidae)	16. Micronesian Scrubfowl *Megapodius laperouse* (Megapodiidae) 15. Wild Turkey *Meleagris gallopavo* (Meleagridae) 14. Grey Tinamou *Tinamus tao* (Tinamidae)
Aquatic birds	1. Greater Flamingo *Phoenicopterus ruber* (Phoenicopteridae) 2. Crowned Crane *Balearica pavonina* (Gruidae) 3. Black-Necked Stilt *Himantopus mexicanus* (Recurvirostrini)	29. Snowy Sheathbill *Chionis alba* (Chionidae) 28. Black-Legged Seriema *Chunga burmeisteri* (Cariamidae) 27. Little Buttonquail *Turnix velox* (Turnicidae)

Preferred Species and Characters

Table 4. (Continued).

Group	The most attractive species	Species perceived as ugly
Terrestrial birds	1. Indigo-banded Kingfisher *Alcedo cyanopecta (Alcedinidae)* 2. Russet-Crowned Motmot *Momotus mexicanus* (Momotidae) 3. Common Hoopoe *Upupa epops* (Upupidae)	25. Willcock's Honeyguide *Indicator willcocksi* (Indicatoridae) 24. Groove-Billed Ani *Crotophaga sulcirostris* (Crotophagidae) 23. Violaceous Coucal *Centropus violaceus* (Centropodidae)
Passerines	1. Blue-and-White Flycatcher *Cyanoptila cyanomelana* (Muscicapini) 2. Blue-Tit *Parus caeruleus* (Parinae) 3. Olive Warbler *Peucedramus taeniatus* (Peucedraminae)	30. Common bananaquit *Coereba flaveola* (Thraupini) 29. Long-Tailed Tit *Aegithalos caudatus* (Aegithalidae) 28. Indian Lark *Mirafra erythroptera* (Alaudidae)
Bassal mammals	1. Common Wombat *Vombatus ursinus* (Vombatidae) 2. Southern Tree Hyrax *Dendrohyrax arboreus* (Procaviidae) 3. Koala *Phascolarctos cinereus* (Phascolarctidae)	35. Duck-billed Platypus *Ornithorhynchus anatinus* (Ornithorhynchidae) 34. Incan Caenolestid *Lestoros inca* (Caenolestidae) 33. Eastern Barred Bandicoot *Perameles gunnii* (Peramelidae)
Glires	1. Alpine Pika *Ochotona alpina* (Ochotonidae) 2. Dassie Rat *Petromus typicus* (Petromuridae) 3. Degu *Octodon degu* (Octodontidae)	33. Lesser Blind Mole Rat *Spalax leucodon* (Spalacidae) 32. Brazilian Porcupine *Coendou prehensilis* (Erethizontidae) 31. Giant Mole-rat *Cryptomys mechowi* (Bathyergidae)
Euarchonta	1. Rondo Bushbaby *Galago rondoensis* (Galagidae) 2. Ravelobe Mouse Lemur *Microcebus ravelobensis* (Microcebinae) 3. Ring-tailed Lemur *Lemur catta* (Lemuridae)	33. Golden Snub-nosed Monkey *Rhinopithecus roxellana* (odd-nosed I former Colobinae*) 32. Proboscis Monkey *Nasalis larvatus* (odd-nosed II, Colobinae*) 31. Pen-tailed Treeshrew *Ptilocercus lowii* (Ptilocercidae)

Table 4. (Continued).

Group	The most attractive species	Species perceived as ugly
Laurasiatheria	1. Red Panda *Ailurus fulgens* (Ailuridae) 2. Long-eared Hedgehog *Hemiechinus auritus* (Erinaceidae) 3. Brown Bear *Ursus arctos* (Ursidae)	33. Cuban Solenodon *Solenodon cubanus* (Solenodontidae) 32. Kouprey *Bos sauveli* (Bovidae) 31. Common Warthog *Phacochoerus africanus* (Suidae)

*Colobinae were split into three separate groups according to Sterner et al. 2006.

Figure 19. Examples of most preferred species within particular higher taxa according to our respondents. Philippine Pitviper (*Parias flavomaculatus*); Lizards: Crotalinae. Original painting by Silvie Lišková.

Figure 20. Examples of most preferred species within particular higher taxa according to our respondents. Coarse Chameleon (*Chamaeleo rudis*); Lizards: Chamaeleoninae. Original painting by Silvie Lišková.

Preferred Species and Characters

Figure 21. Examples of most preferred species within particular higher taxa according to our respondents. Spotted Turtle (Clemmys guttata); Turtles: Emydinae. Original painting by Silvie Lišková.

Figure 22. Examples of most preferred species within particular higher taxa according to our respondents. Brown Kiwi (*Apteryx australis*); Basal birds: Apterigidae. Original painting by Silvie Lišková.

Figure 23. Examples of most preferred species within particular higher taxa according to our respondents. Greater Flamingo (*Phoenicopterus ruber*); Aquatic birds: Phoenicopteridae. Original painting by Silvie Lišková.

Figure 24. Examples of most preferred species within particular higher taxa according to our respondents. Indigo-banded Kingfisher (Alcedo cyanopecta); Terrestrial birds: Alcedinidae. Original painting by Silvie Lišková.

Figure 25. Examples of most preferred species within particular higher taxa according to our respondents. Blue-and-White Flycatcher (Cyanoptila cyanomelana); Passeriformes: Muscicapini. Original painting by Silvie Lišková.

Figure 26. Examples of most preferred species within particular higher taxa according to our respondents. Common Wombat (Vombatus ursinus); Basal mammals: Vombatidae. Original painting by Silvie Lišková.

Figure 27. Examples of most preferred species within particular higher taxa according to our respondents. Alpine Pika (*Ochotona alpina*); Glires: Ochotonidae. Original painting by Silvie Lišková.

Figure 28. Examples of most preferred species within particular higher taxa according to our respondents. Rondo Bushbaby (Galago rondoensis); Euarchonta: Galagidae. Original painting by Silvie Lišková.

Figure 29. Examples of most preferred species within particular higher taxa according to our respondents. Red Panda (Ailurus fulgens); Laurasiatheria: Ailuridae. Original painting by Silvie Lišková.

Figure 30. Examples of most preferred species within particular higher taxa according to our respondents. Royal Antelope (Neotragus pygmaeus); Antelopes and allies (Bovidae). Original painting by Silvie Lišková.

48 D. Frynta, J. Marešová, E. Landová et al.

The preferred traits varied greatly from set to set. Obviously, contribution of coloration on human preferences was important among birds (see Bennett & Owens 2002 for evolution of bird coloration) and reptiles, while it was only marginal among mammals characterized by limited variance in this character (for evolution of mammalian coloration see Caro 2005). We further discuss the observed patterns group by group.

SNAKES

The preferred snakes were those with bright background colors: green as Philippine pitviper (*Parias flavomaculatus*, Crotalinae), red as coral earth snake (*Geophis semidoliatus*, Dipsadinae) and coral cylinder snakes *Anilius scytale* (Aniliinae), and bluish as colubrine *Laticauda colubrina* (Laticaudinae). Also stripes or disruptive pattern contributed to beauty. The plain grey or brownish species with snake-typical body plan were placed in the middle of preference scale. Species without clearly differed head and tail were perceived as unattractive: Brongersma's worm snake (*Typhlops brongersmianus,* Typhlopinae), *Liotyphlops beuii* (Anomalepinae), western threadsnake (*Leptotyphlos humilis*, Leptotyphlopinae), Peters' Philippine earth snake(*Rhinophis pillippinus*, Uropeltinae) or southeastern crowned snake (*Tantilla coronata*, Colubrinae).

LIZARDS AND TUATARAS

Our respondents preferred green species irrespective to their morphology: coarse chameleon (*Chameleo rudis,* Chameleonidae), Anzamala Madagascar Shift (*Oplurus fierinensis*, Oplurinae), and terrestrial arboreal alligator lizard (*Abronia graminea*, Gerrhonotinae). Species exhibiting whatever distinct color pattern in combination with lizards-typical body plan as were also preferred. Interestingly, those labeled by respondents as "strange" or "fanciful" were perceived as less attractive, e.g. tuatara (*Sphenodon punctatus,* Sphenodontidae), northern leaf-tail gecko (*Saltuarius cornutus,* Diplodactylinae), Egyptian mastigure (*Uromastyx aegyptia*, Leiolepinae) or Boulenger's pygmy chameleon (*Rhampholeon boulengeri*, Brookesiinae). The animals with reduced limbs as Deraniyagala's tree skink (*Lankascincus deraniyagalai,* Scincinae), Cope's galliwasp (*Celestus stenurus,* Diploglossinae), slender glass lizard (*Ophisaurus atennuatus*, Anguinae) or even worm-like body plan as checkerboard worm lizard (*Trogonophis wiegmani,* Trogonophidae), exmouth worm-lizard (*Aprasia rostrata,* Pygopodinae), blind lizard (*Dibamus bogadeki,* Dibaminae) and California legless lizard *(Anniella pulchra,* Annielinae) were perceived as unattractive or ugly.

TESTUDINES

The most preferred ones were turtles and tortoises with yellow or red pattern on carapax and/or on the head: .spotted turtle (*Clemmys guttata,* Emydinae), Madagascan tortoise (*Astrochelys yniphora,* Testudininae), snail-eating turtle (*Malayemys subrijuga,* Batagurinae), red-headed Amazon side-necked turtle (*Podocnemis erythrocephala,* Podocnemidinae), Florida redbelly turtle (*Pseudemys nelsoni,* Deirochelyinae), three-banded box turtle (*Cuora trifasciata,* Geoemydinae). The list of top ten includes also marine turtles and pig-nosed turtle (*Carettochelis insculpta,* Caretochelinae) with similar appearance. The species placed at the end of the preference scale were labeled by most respondents as "strange" as South-American snake-headed turtle (*Hydromedusa tectifera,* Hydromedusinae) and soft-shelled turtles or "dangerous" and "hostile" as big-headed turtle (*Platysternon megacephalum,* Platysterninae), common snapping turtle (*Chelydra serpentina,* Chelidrinae), or *Staurotypus triporcatus* (Staurotypinae). This feeling of potential danger corresponds also with opinion of many proficient breeders (Figure 9.).

BASAL BIRDS

Favorites of this set were: kiwi (Apteryx australis, Apterygidae), pigeons especially the species with green feathers e.g. Stephan's dove Chalcophaps stephani, negros fruit-dove Ptilinopus arcanus, Sumatran green pigeon Treron oxyura (Columbidae). The species belonging to families Tetraonidae and Anatidae were highly preferred too. The lengths of legs e.g. in lesser rhea (Rhea pennata, Rheidae), ostrich (Struthio camelus, Struthionidae), , northern screamer (Chauna chavaria, Anhimidae) and long tail, e.g., in great argus (Argusianus argus, Phasianidae) or crest as in scaled quail (Callipepla squamata, Odontophoridae) and cassowary (Casuarius casuarius, Casuariidae), are the other observable features increasing the attractiveness of the species/family for humans.

AQUATIC BIRDS

Elegance of shape and length of neck, legs and prominent beaks are the traits of species/families ranked as the most beautiful. Species with short neck, relatively shorter legs and beaks were perceived as unattractive. In this set of pictures, coloration had no marked effect on human ranking.

TERRESTRIAL BIRDS

Coloration of birds is the most important feature for human aesthetic preference. Brightly colored (blue, red, and green) species from different families were perceived as the most beautiful: e.g. indigo-banded kingfisher *Alcedo cyanopecta,* white-throated kingfisher *Halcyon smyrnensis* (Alcedinidae), russet-crowned motmot (*Momotus mexicanus*, Momotidae) or red-and-green macaw (*Ara chloropterus*, Psittacidae). Also prominent beak (in e.g. Boehm's bee-eater (*Merops boehmi,* Meropidae), Emerald toucanet (*Aulacorhynchus prasinus*, Ramphastinae), great jacamar (*Jacamerops aureus*, Galbulidae) and/or crest e.g. in common hoopoe (*Upupa epops*,Upupidae,) shift the species upwards on the preference scale (Figure 12.). The combination of bright coloration with prominent beak and crest evoke positive emotions reliably. The lengths of the legs or tail are not important.

PASSERINES

Brightly colored birds with blue e.g. blue waxbill (*Uraeginthus angolensis* Estrildinae), blue-tit (*Parus caerules,* Parinae), blue-and-white flycatcher (*Cyanoptila cyanomelana,* Muscicapini), red e.g. Crimson sunbird (*Aethopyga siparaja,* Nectariniidae), green and yellow or orange colures are perceived as the most beautiful. The black mask on a head e.g. in olive warbler (*Peucedramus taeniatus,* Peucedraminae), village weaver (*Ploceus cucullatus*, Ploceinae) also enhances preferences to the holder. However, the congruence among respondents is low. Probably, human's cognitive abilities are not adjusted to recognize and classify passerines with such uniform morphology.

Preferred Species and Characters

BASAL MAMMALS

Characterization of three most preferred basal mammals, i.e., common wombat (*Vombatus ursinus,* Vombatidae), southern tree hyrax (*Dendrohyrax arboreus,* Procaviidae) and *Phascolarctos cinereus* (Phascolarctidae) is quite simple – they all have appearance of lovely Teddy bears with dense fur, shaggy round ears and relatively big eyes. The animals possessing long and shaggy tail as northern tamandua (*Tamandua mexicana,* Myrmecophagidae), yellow-footed rock-wallaby *Petrogale xanthopus* (Macropodidae), squirrel glider *Petaurus norfolcensis* (Petauridae).are preferred too. Interestingly, elephant (*Loxodonta africana*) occupies just the eighth position on the scale of preferences. Subterranean, mouse-like animals and duck-billed platypus are placed on the tail of humans' preferences.

GLIRES

This set of the pictures was unpopular among our respondents. Some students even tried to avoid evaluation of this set and expressed wisdom to arrange sets consisting of other animals. Most preferred species resemble approximately "Mickey Mouse" body scheme e.g. Alpine pika (*Ochotona alpina,* Ochotonidae), degu (*Octodon degu,* Octodontidae) or lesser big-footed mouse (*Macrotarsomys bastardi,* Nesomyidae). The length shaggy tail, big ears and bigger body size are preferred traits in this group. As in the previous group, the subterranean species e.g. giant mole-rat (*Cryptomys mechowi,* Bathyergidae) or lesser blind mole rat (*Spalax leucodon,* Spalacidae) and those resembling rat were unequivocally perceived as ugly.

EUARCHONTA

It is obvious that respondents prefer small nocturnal species with big eyes and ears e.g. rondo bush baby (*Galago rondoensis,* Galagidae), ravelobe mouse lemur *(Microcebus ravelobensis,* Microcebinae) or slow lori (*Nycticebus coucang,* Lorisidae). The primates with long and shaggy tail, e.g., ring-tailed lemur (*Lemur catta,* Lemuridae), Milne-Edwards's (*Propithecus edwardsi,* Indridae), golden lion tamarin (*Leontopithecus rosalia,* Leontopithecina, Calitrichidae) or collared titi (*Callicebus torquatus,* Pitheciidae) are highly preferred too, similarly as in other groups (see above Basal mammals and Glires). Surprisingly, great apes represented by orang-outan (*Pongo abelii,* Hominidae) were placed to thirteenth position only on preference scale. The species placed at the end of the preference scale were in some aspect different from apish typical appearance e.g. pen-tailed tree-shrew *Ptilocercus lowii* (Ptilocercidae), proboscis monkey (*Nasalis larvatus,* Colobinae).

LAURASIATHERIA

In these set again bear-like animals as red panda (*Ailurus fulgens*, Ailuridae) or really bears brown bear (*Ursus arctos*, Ursidae) were preferred. Again species with dense fur, shaggy round ears animals long-eared hedgehog (*Hemiechinus auritus*, Erinaceidae) and/or apparent color pattern e.g. leopard (*Leopardus pardalis,* Felidae) or giraffe (*Giraffa camelopardalis*, Giraffidae) were perceived as charming or beautiful. For the list of unattractive species see Table 4.

CONCLUSION

Worldwide net of zoos supports considerable proportions of living species, at least in the case of terrestrial vertebrates as mammals, birds and reptiles. This collection may play role of valuable Noah's Ark providing that following conditions are fullfilled.

1) It is reasonable selection of species to keep that may help to cover all major clades and species/taxa under the most apparent risk of extinction. This requires application of both phylogenetic approach and actual information on conservation status of concerned species.

2) It is necessary to reflect the fact that economics and space essentially limits the size of zoo populations. We clearly demonstrated that zoo populations of most species (including those actually going to extinction in nature) are too small to be sustainable even in the short-time perspecive. Thus management of these insufficient populations should be promptly introduced to this alarming situation. This especially requires blurring boundaries between captive and wild populations (cf. Dickie et al. 2007) as well as those between zoo animals and populations kept by other respectable breeders (including private and NGO collections). Surplus animals in zoos should not be further castrated or killed as dictated by defenders of animal rights and wellfare ethics, but preferably moved from hard core of studbook populations kept in zoos and professional breeders into its periphery, e.g., private breeders, NGOs, reintroduction programs, etc. Simultaneously, priming, coordination and methodical role of zoos and their breeding programs should be extended. Conservation ethics (Hutchins 2007) evaluating survival of the species as

moral priority have to be used to overcome administrative barriers and popular preconceptions.

3) Decisions, which species is the right one to keep and breed in large numbers, have to follow conservation needs rather than popularity of the species. Only 187 out of 23,582 living species of higher vertebrates have worldwide zoo population exceeding 500 specimens. Even more alarming is that only 49 out of these 187 species are those actually endangered.

We confirmed that zoo collections are biased in favor of the birds (higher numer of captive species) and mammals (larger population sizes), while reptiles are underrepresented. Thorough analyses of zoo population sizes suggest that body size is without any doubt the most prominent factor increasing the representation of given species or higher taxon in zoos. Although large animals are disproportionally more expensive to keep they are frequently preferred, probably due to visitor's preferrence.

In addition to body size, there is appearance of the animal per se. Some animals are perceived as more attractive than the others. Our respondents were exposed to the sets of pictures depicting different animal species and asked to rank the species according to their beauty. We were surprised by the high degree of congruence among the responses of different persons. Nevertheless, the characters contributing to human preferences varied greatly among studied sets of pictures. Conspicuous coloration was prominent factor in some birds and reptiles taxa, while preferred body proportions varied among studied taxa. Most comparisons carried out among related species showed the strong effects of beauty on size of zoo populations. In contrast, when not species, but families/subfamilies were compared this effect has remained significant within particular animal taxon only (basal mammals, Laurasiatheria, terrestrial birds). Obviously, characters matching human aesthetic criteria are distributed across different animal taxa. Thus, human preferences towards particular species belonging to the same family/subfamily may sometimes differ considerably. This may help zoos to find the species satisfying aesthetic criteria of the visitors and keepers in almost every clade of animals worth of ex situ conservation effort.

ACKNOWLEDGMENTS

The research was supported by the Grant Agency of the Czech Academy of Sciences (projects IAA6111410 and IAA 6011410803); personal costs of J.M.

were covered by the Czech Science Foundation (project 206/05/H012) and those of E.L. by the Czech Ministry of Education, Youth and Sports (project MSMT 6007665806).

REFERENCES

Areekul, B. & Quicke, D. L. J. (2006). *The use of colour characters in phylogenetic reconstruction.* Biological Journal of Linnean Society, 88, 193-202.

Baenninger, R. (1988). *Animals in Art: Some Trends Across Three Millennia.* The Journal of psychology, 122, 183-191.

Baker, A. (2007). *Animal ambassadors: an analysis of the effectiveness and conservation impact of ex situ breeding efforts.* In Zimmermann, & M. Hatchwell, & A. D. Lesley, & C. West (Eds.), Zoos in the 21st Century. Catalysts for Conservation? (pp. 139-155). New York, NY: Cambridge University Press.

Balmford, A. (2000). *Separating fact from artfact in analyses of zoo visitor preferences.* Conservation Biology, 14(4), 1193-1195.

Barker, F. K. & Cibois, A. & Schikler, P. & Einstein, J. & Cracraft, J. (2004). *Phylogeny and diversification of the largest avian radiation.* Proceedings of the National Academy of Science, 101(30), 11040-11045.

Barkow, J. H., & Cosmides, L., & Tooby, J., (1992). *The Adapted Mind.* New York, NY: Oxford University Press.

Bennett, P. M., & Owens, I. P. F. (2002). *Evolutionary Ecology of Birds.* New York, NY: Oxford University Press.

Berlin, B. (1992). *Ethnobiological classification: principles of categorization of plants and animals in traditional societies.* Princeton, NJ: Princeton University Press.

Bertolero, A. & Oro, D. & Besnard, A. (2007). *Assessing the efficacy of reintroduction programmes by modelling adult survival: the example of Hermann's tortoise.* Animal Conservation, 10, 360-368.

Bininda-Emonds, O. R. P. & Cardillo, M. & Jones, K. E. & MacPhee, R. D. E. & Beck, R. M. D. & Grenyer, R. & Price, S. A., & Vos, R.A. & Gittleman, J. L. & Purvis, A. (2007). *The delayed rise of present-day mammals.* Nature, 446, 507-512.

Brighsmith, D. & Hilburn, J. & Campo, A. & Boyd, J. & Frisius, R. & Janik, D. & Guilen (2005). *The use of hand-raised psittacines for reintroduction: a case study of scarlet macaws (Ara macao) in Peru and Costa Rica.* Biological Conservation, 121, 465-472.

Brown, M. & Perrin, M. & Hoffman, B. (2007). *Reintroduction of captive-bred African Grass-Owls Tyto capensis into natural habitat.* Ostrich, 78(1), 75-79.

Caro, T. M. & Graham, C. M. & Stoner, C. J. & Flores, M. M. (2003). *Correlates of horn and antler shape in bovids and cervids.* Behavioral Ecology and Sociobiology, 55, 32-41.

Caro, T. M. (2005). *The adaptive significance of coloration in mammals.* Bioscience, 55(2), 125-136.

Chiari, Y. & Vences, M. & Vieites, D. R. & Rabemananjara, F. & Bora, P. & Ramilijaona Ravoahanangimalala, O. & Meyer, A. (2004). *New evidence for parallel evolution of colour patterns in Malagasy poison frogs. (Mantella).* Molecular Ecology, 13, 3763-3774.

Cohn, J. P. (1992). *Decisions at the zoo: Ethics, politics and animal rights concerns affect the process of balancing conservation goals and the public interests.* BioScience, 42(9), 654-659.

Connolly, J. D. & Cree, A. (2008). *Risks of a late start to captive management for conservation: Phenotypic differences between wild and captive individuals of a viviparous endangered scink (Oligosoma otagense).* Biological Conservation, 141, 1283-1292.

Czech, B. & Krausman, P. R. & Borkhataria, R. (1998*). Social Construction, Political Power, and Allocation of Benefits to Endangered Species.* Conservation Biology, 12(5), 1103-1112.

Davey, G. C. L. & McDonald, A. S. & Hrisave, U. & Prabhu, G. G. & Iwawaki, S. & Jim, C. I. & Merckelbach, H. & de Jong, P. J. & Leung, P. W. L. & Reimann, B. C. (1998). *A cross-cultural study of animal fears.* Behaviour Research and Therapy, 36, 735-750.

del Hoyo, J., & Elliot, A., & Sargatal, J. (Eds.) (1992-2002). *Handbook of the Birds of the World (Volumes 1-7).* Barcelona, Spain: Lynx Edicions.

Denton, J.S. & Hitchings, P. S. & Beebee, T. J. C. & Gent, A. (1997). *A recovery program for the natterjack toad (Bufo calamita).* Conservation biology, 11(6), 1329-1338.

Dickie, L. A., & Bonner, J.P., & West, C. (2007). *In situ conservation and ex situ conservation: blurring the boundaries between zoos and the wild.* In Zimmermann, & M. Hatchwell, & A. D. Lesley, & C. West (Eds.), Zoos in the 21st Century. Catalysts for Conservation? (pp. 220-236). New York, NY: Cambridge University Press.

Ericson, P. G. P. & Anderson, C. L. & Britton, T. & Elzanowski, A. & Johansson, U. S. & Källersjo, M. & Ohlson, J. I. & Parson, J. T. & Zuccon, D. & Mayer,

G. (2006). *Diversification of Neoaves: integration of molecular sequence data and fossils.* Biology Letters, 2, 543-547.

Field, D.A., & Dickie, L.A. (2007). *Zoo coalitions for conservations.* In Zimmermann, & M. Hatchwell, & A. D. Lesley, & C. West (Eds.), Zoos in the 21st Century. Catalysts for Conservation? (pp. 287-303). New York, NY: Cambridge University Press.

Frankham, R., & Ballou, J. D., & Briscoe, D. A. (2002). *Introduction to conservation genetics.* Cambridge, UK: Cambridge University Press.

Frankham, R. (2008). *Genetic adaptation to captivity in species conservation programs.* Molecular Ecology, 17, 325-333.

Goodman, M. & Porter, C. A. & Czelusniak, J. & Page, L. C. & Schneider, H. & Shoshani, J. & Gunnell, G. & Groves, C. P. (1998). *Toward a phylogenetic classification of primates based on DNA evidence complemented by fossil evidence.* Molecular Phylogenetics and Evolution, 9(3), 585-598.

Gould, S. J. (1979). *Mickey Mouse meets Konrad Lorenz.* Natural History, 88(5), 30-34.

Gunnthorsdottir, A. (2001). *Physical attractiveness of an animal species as a decision factor for its preservation.* Anthrozoos, 14(4), 204-215.

Guthrie, R. D. (2005). *The nature of Paleolithic art.* Chicago, IL: University of Chicago Press.

Hackett, S. J., & Kimball, R. T. & Reddi, S. & Bowie, R. C. K. & Braun, E. L. & Braun, M. J. & Chojnowski, J. L. & Cox, A. W. & Han, K. L. & Harshman, J. & Huddleston, C. J. & Marks, B. D. & Miglia, K. J. & Moore, W. S. & Sheldon, F. H. & Steadman, D. W. & Witt, C. C. & Yuri, T. (2008). *Phylogenomic study of birds reveals their evolutionary history.* Science, 320(27), 1763-1768.

Halberstadt, J. & Rhodes, G. (2003). *It's not just average faces that are attractive: Computer-manipulated averageness makes birds, fish and automobiles attractive.* Psychonomic Bulletin and Review, 10(1), 149-156.

Hale, K. A. & Briskie, J. V. (2007). *Challenges to understanding the consequences of population bottlenecks for the conservation of endangered wildlife.* Animal Conservation, 10, 19-21.

Herzog, H.A. & Bentley, A. & Hahn, M. W. (2004). *Random drift and large shifts in popularity of dog breeds.* Proceedings of Royal Society Series B Biology, 271, S353-S356.

Holst, B., & Dickie L.A. (2007). *How do national and international regulations and policies influence the role of zoos and aquariums in conservation?* In A. Zimmermann, & M. Hatchwell, & A. D. Lesley, & C. West (Eds.), Zoos in the 21st Century. Catalysts for Conservation? (pp. 22-37). New York, NY: Cambridge University Press.

Hosey, G. (2008). *A preliminary model of human-animal relationships in zoos.* Applied Animal Behaviour Science, 109, 105-127.

Hutchins, M. (2007). *The animal rights-conservation debate: can zoos and aquariums play a role?* In A. Zimmermann, & M. Hatchwell, & A. D. Lesley, & C. West (Eds.), Zoos in the 21st Century. Catalysts for Conservation? (pp. 92-110). New York, NY: Cambridge University Press.

International Species Information System *(ISIS) database* (2008). URL: http://www.isis.org

IUCN (2008). *IUCN Red List of Threatened Species.* World Conservation Union, URL: http://www.iucnredlist.org

Jule, K. L. & Leaver, L. A. & Lea, S. E. G. (2008). *The effects of captive experience on reintroduction survival in carnivores: A review and analysis.* Biological Conservation, 141, 355-363.

Kellert, S. R. (1985): *Social and Perceptual Factors in the Preservation of Animal Species.* Journal of Wildlife Management, 49(2), 528-536.

Kimura, M. (1983). *The neutral theory of molecular evolution.* Cambridge, UK: Cambridge University Press.

Lande, R. (1999). *Extinction risks from anthropogenic, ecological, and genetics factors.* In Landweber, L. F. & Dobson, A. P. (Eds.), Genetics and the extinction of species: DNA and the conservation of biodiversity. (pp. 1-23) Princeton, NJ: Princeton University Press.

Leader-Williams, N., & Balmford, A., & Linkie, M., & Mace, G.M., & Smith, R.J., & Stevenson, M., & Walter, O., & West, C. & Zimmerman,A. (2007). *Beyond the ark: conservation biologists' views of the achievements of zoos in conservation.* In Zimmermann, & M. Hatchwell, & A. D. Lesley, & C. West (Eds.), Zoos in the 21st Century. Catalysts for Conservation? (pp. 236-257). New York, NY: Cambridge University Press.

Lewis-Williams, J. D. (2002). *The Mind in the Cave: Consciousness and the Origins of Art. London, UK:* Thames & Hudson.

Marešová, J. & Frynta, D. (2008). *Noah's Ark is full of common species attractive to humans: the case of boid snakes in Zoos.* Ecological Economics, 64, 554-558.

Marešová, J. & Frynta, D. (2009). *We all appreciate the same animals: cross-cultural comparison of human aesthetic preferences for snake species in Papua New Guinea and Europe.* Ethology, in press.

Masi, A. (1996). *Birds: DNA Sibley's Sequence.* URL: http://www.scricciolo.com/classificazione/ sibley's_index.htm

Conclusion 59

McDougall, P. T. & Réale, D. & Sol, D. & Reader, S. M. (2006). *Wildlife conservation and animal temperament: causes and consequences of evolutionary change for captive, reintroduced, and wild populations.* Animal Conservation, 9, 39-48.

Metrick, A. & Weitzman, M. L. (1996). *Patterns of behaviour in endangered species preservation.* Land Economics, 72(1), 1-16.

Metrick, A. & Weitzman, M. L. (1998). *Conflict and choices in biodiversity preservations.* Journal of Economic Perspectives, 12(3), 21-35.

Morris, D. (1967). *The naked ape.* New York, NY: McGraw-Hill.

Murphy, W. J. & Eizirik, E. & Johnson, W. E. & Zhang, Y. P. & Ryder, O. A. & O'Brien, S. J. (2001). *Molecular phylogenetics and the origin of placental mammals.* Nature, 409, 614-618.

O'Regan, H. J. & Kitchener, A. C. (2005). *The effects of captivity on morphology of captive, domesticated and feral mammals.* Mammal Review, 35(3-4), 215-230.

Pielou, E. C., (1966). *The measurement of diversity in different types of biological collections.* Journal of Theoretical Biology, 13, 131–144.

Pittenger, J. B. (1990). *Body proportions as information for age and cuteness: Animals in illustrated childrens books.* Perception and Psychophysics, 42(2), 124-130.

Price, M. R. S., & Fa J. E. (2007). *Reintroductions from zoos: a conservation guiding light or a shooting star?* In Zimmermann, & M. Hatchwell, & A. D. Lesley, & C. West (Eds.), Zoos in the 21st Century. Catalysts for Conservation? (pp. 155-178). New York, NY: Cambridge University Press.

Quinn, P. C. & Kelly, D. J. & Lee, K. & Pascalis, O. & Slater, A. M (2008). *Preference for attractive faces in human infants extends beyond conspecifics.* Developmental Science, 11(1), 76-83.

Raup, D. M. (1991). *Extinction: Bad genes or bad luck?* New York, NY: W.W. Norton and Company.

Reed, D. H. & Nicholas, A. C. & Stratton, G. E. (2007). *Genetic quality of individuals impacts population dynamics.* Animal Conservation, 10, 275-283.

Rodrígez-Clarc, K. M. (1999). *Genetic theory and evidence supporting current practices in captive breeding for conservation.* In Landweber, L. F. & Dobson, A. P. (Eds.), Genetics and the extinction of species: DNA and the conservation of biodiversity. (pp. 47–73) Princeton, NJ: Princeton University Press.

Samples, K. C. & Dixon, J. A. & Gowen, M. M. (1986). *Information Disclosure and Endangered Species Valuation.* Land Economics, 62(3), 306-312.

Schmidt-Nielsen, K. (1984). *Scaling: Why Is Animal Size So Important?* Cambridge, UK: Cambridge University Press.

Seddon, P. J. & Soorae, P. S. & Launay, F. (2005). *Taxonomic bias in reintroduction projects.* Animal Conservation, 8, 51-58.

Shannon, C. D. (1963): *The mathematical theory of communication.* Urbana/Chicago, IL: University of Illinois Press.

Sheldon, A.L. (1969). *Equitability indices: dependence on the species count.* Ecology, 50, 466-467.

Sibley, C. G., & Alquist, J. E. (1990). *Phylogeny and classification of birds: a study in molecular evolution.* New Haven, CT: Yale University Press.

Sibley, C. G. & Monroe, B. L. (1990). *Distribution and taxonomy of birds of the world.* New Haven, CT: Yale University Press.

Sibley, C. G. & Monroe, B. L. (1993). *A supplement to 'Distribution and taxonomy of birds of the world'.* New Haven, CT: Yale University Press.

Simon, B. M. & Leff, C. S. & Doerksen, H. (1995). *Allocating scarce resources for endangered species recovery.* Journal of Policy Analysis and Management, 14(3), 415-432.

Soulé, M. E. (1980). *Thresholds for survival: maintaining fitness and evolutionary potential.* In: Soulé, M. E. & Wilcox, B. A. (Eds.), Conservation Biology: An evolutionary-ecological perspective (pp. 151-169). Sunderland, MA: Sinauer.

Soulé, M. E. & Gilpin, M. & Conway, W. & Foose, T. (1986). *The millennium ark: how long a voyage, how many staterooms, how many passengers?* Zoo Biology, 5, 101-113.

StatSoft Inc. (2001). *STATISTICA (data analysis software system), vers.6.0.,* URL: http://www.statsoft.com.

Sterling, E., & Lee, J., & Wood, T. (2007). *Conservation education in zoos: an emphasis on behavioral change.* In A. Zimmermann, & M. Hatchwell, & A. D. Lesley, & C. West (Eds.), Zoos in the 21st Century. Catalysts for Conservation? (pp. 37-51). New York, NY: Cambridge University Press.

Sterner, K. N. & Raaum, R. L. & Zhang Y. P. & Steward, C. B. & Disotell, T. D. (2006). *Mitochondrial data support and odd-nosed colobine clade.* Molecular Phylogenetics and Evolution, 40, 1-7.

Stokes, D. L. (2007). Things We Like: *Human Preferences among Similar Organisms and Implications for Conservation.* Human Ecology, 35, 361-369.

Taberlet, P. & Valentini, A. & Rezaei, H. R. & Naderi, S. & Pompanon, F. & Negrini, R. & Ajmone-Marsan, P. (2008). *Are cattle, sheep, and goats endangered species?* Molecular Ecology, 17, 275-284.

Taylor, S. S. & Jamieson, I. G. & Armstrong, D. P. (2005). *Successful island reintroductions of New Zealand robins and saddlebacks with small number of founders.* Animal Conservation, 8, 415-420.

The BirdLife Taxonomic Working Group (BTWG) (2008). *The BirdLife Checklist, May 2008, mainly based on Sibley and Monroe (1990, 1993) and others taxonomic sources. URL:* http://www.birdlife.org/datazone/species/taxonomy.html

Towsend, T. M. & Larson, A. & Louis, E. & Macey, J. (2004). *Molecular phylogenetics of Squamata: The position of snakes, amphisbaenians and dibamids, and roots of squamale tree.* Systematic Biology, 53, 737-757.

Traill, L. W. & Bradshaw, C. J. A. & Brook, B. W. (2007). *Minimum viable population size: A meta-analysis of 30 years of published estimates.* Biological Conservation, 139, 159-166.

Tudge, C. (1995). *Captive audiences for future conservation.* New Scientist, 145(1962), 51-52.

Uetz, P. et al (2008). *The TIGR Reptile Database, URL: http://www.reptile-database.org.* Peter Uetz and German Herpetological Society (DGHT), Heidelberg, Germany, accesed May 23, 2006

Van Hook, T. (1997). *Insect coloration and implication for conservation.* Florida Entomologist, 80(2), 193-210.

Vidal, N. & Hedges, B. S. (2005). *The phylogeny of squamate reptiles (lizards, snakes and amphisbaenians) inferred from nine nuclear protein-coding genes.* C. R. Biologies, 328, 1001-1008.

Ward, P. I. & Mosberger, N. & Kistler, C. & Fischer, O. (1998). *The relationship between popularity and body size in zoo animals.* Conservation Biology, 12, 1408-1411.

White, T. H. Jr. & Collazo, J. A. & Viella, J. F. (2005). *Survival of captive-reared puerto rican parrots released in the caribbean national forest.* Condor, 107, 424-432.

Wilson, D. E., & Reeder, D. A. M. (Eds.) (2005). *Mammal species of the world: A taxonomic and geographic reference (3rd ed).* Johns Hopkins, University Press, 2,142 pp. Checklist available on: http://nmnhgoph.si.edu/msw/

Wilson, E. O. (1992). *The diversity of life.* Cambridge, MA: Harvard University Press.

Wilson, E. O. (2002). *The future of life.* New York, NY: Alfred A. Knopf

ABOUT THE AUTHORS

The authors are from the Ecology and Ethology Group, Department of Zoology, Faculty of Science, Charles University, Viničná 7, CZ-128 44 Praha 2, Czech Republic. The corresponding authors e-mail: frynta@centrum.cz

INDEX

A

accidental, xii
accommodation, xii
adaptations, xi, 57
addax, xi
administrative, 54
adult, 55
aesthetic criteria, ix, 54
age, 59
allies, 2, 17, 18, 19, 39, 47
Amazon, 49
ambassadors, 55
amphibians, xiii, 3,
animals, i, iii, v, xi, xii, xiii, xiv, 1, 2, 4, 7, 8, 16, 17, 39, 48, 51, 52, 53, 54, 55, 58, 59, 61
anthropogenic, 58
application, 53
arousal, 15, 17
Asia, iii
assessment, 39
attractiveness, ix, xiii, xiv, 2, 16, 18, 23, 24, 25, 26, 27, 28, 29, 30, 31, 32, 33, 34, 35, 36, 49, 57
automobiles, 57

B

barriers, 54
behavioral change, 60
bias, xii, xiv, 60
biodiversity, 4, 5, 21, 58, 59
biota, xii
birds, xii, xiv, 1, 3, 4, 5, 8, 11, 12, 13, 21, 22, 23, 27, 28, 29, 30, 31, 40, 41, 43, 44, 48, 50, 53, 54, 57, 60
bison, xi
blood, 8, 15
blurring, 8, 53, 56
boas, xiii, 2, 15
body size, ix, xiii, xiv, 2, 15, 16, 17, 18, 19, 22, 23, 25, 26, 28, 29, 30, 32, 34, 35, 36, 51, 54, 61
bottlenecks, 7, 57
Brazilian, 41
breeding, ix, xi, xii, 2, 7, 11, 16, 53, 55, 59

C

captive populations, xi, xii, 5, 8
case study, 56
categorization, 55
cattle, 60

circuses, xi
classes, xiv, 5, 11, 21
classification, 55, 57, 60
coalitions, 57
coding, 61
cognitive abilities, 50
colors, 48
communication, 60
communities, 4
competition, xii
composition, xii
condor, xi
congress, vi
congruence, 2, 50, 54
conservation, ix, xii, xiii, 2, 3, 7, 8, 11, 16, 22, 53, 54, 55, 56, 57, 58, 59, 61
conspicuous coloration, xiii
construction, xiii
control, 3
coral, 48
correlation, 16, 17
costs, xii, 3, 54
covering, 1
cross-cultural, xiv, 56, 58
cross-cultural comparison, 58
culture, xii, xiv

D

danger, 49
data analysis, 60
database, 1, 3, 58, 61
decision making, xii, 18
decisions, xiii
degradation, 7
demographic factors, 8
density, 8
dependent variable, 22
depression, 8
deviation, 22
diploid, 7
disaster, xi

distribution, xiii, 7, 12, 13
diversification, 55
diversity, xii, 4, 5, 11, 59, 61
DNA, 57, 58, 59
dogs, xii

E

ears, 51, 52
earth, 48
eating, 40, 49
ecological, 58, 60
Ecological Economics, 58
ecology, 4, 8
economics, 53
education, 55
elater, 34
election, 22
elephant, 51
e-mail, 63
emotions, xii, 15, 17, 39, 50
endangered species, ix, xi, xii, xiv, 11, 12, 13, 59, 60
environment, xii
ethics, 53
ethnobiologists, xii
Europe, xiv, 58
evolution, 37, 48, 56, 58, 60
extinction, xi, 7, 8, 11, 21, 53, 58, 59
eyes, 51

F

family, ix, 2, 15, 17, 21, 22, 23, 24, 25, 26, 27, 28, 29, 30, 31, 32, 33, 34, 35, 36, 49, 54
farms, xi
fear, xii, 56
federal government, xiii
ferret, xi
fish, xiii, 57
fitness, 60
fluctuations, xii

Index

fossil, 57
funding, xiii, 9
FWS, xiii

G

generation, 8
genes, 59, 61
genetic drift, 8
genetics, 57, 58
glass, 48
goals, 56
goose, xi, 1
government, vi, xiii
gracilis, 15
groups, ix, xiii, 3, 21, 22, 23, 24, 27, 37, 39, 42, 52

H

habitat, 4, 56
herbivores, xii
homogenous, 16, 21, 37
horse, xi, 1
hotels, xii
human, ix, xii, xiii, xiv, 2, 4, 11, 15, 16, 17, 18, 22, 23, 37, 39, 40, 48, 49, 50, 51, 54, 58, 59
human will, xiii
hunter-gatherers, xii

I

inbreeding, xi, 8
inclusion, ix
Indian, 15, 17, 40, 41
indices, 5, 60
infants, 59
Information System, 1, 58
injury, vi
institutions, 2
insurance, xi
integration, 57

island, 61
IUCN, 1, 11, 12, 13, 16, 17, 18, 58

L

legislation, 8
life style, 22

M

maintenance, xi, 7, 8
mammals, xii, xiii, xiv, 1, 3, 4, 5, 8, 11, 12, 13, 22, 24, 33, 41, 45, 48, 51, 52, 53, 54, 55, 56, 59
management, 53, 56
mask, 37, 50
measurement, 59
media, 2
median, 4, 7, 23, 24
mental capacity, xii
meta-analysis, 61
metabolism, 3
Mexican, 40
micronesian, 40
Ministry of Education, 55
misinterpretation, 8
models, 2, 22
Modern Age, xii
mole, 51
morphology, xi, 16, 48, 50, 59
mouse, 1, 51
multiple regression, 23
mutations, 8

N

natural, 5, 56
neck, 50
negative emotions, xii
network, 4, 11
NGOs, xiii, 53
normal, 7

normal distribution, 7
nose, 49
nuclear, 61

O

oat, 1
olive, 15, 50
oryx, xi

P

Pacific, 40
PCA, 2
perceived attractiveness, xiii, xiv, 2, 23, 24
phylogenetic, 21, 37, 53, 55, 57
phylogeny, 21, 61
pig, 1, 49
placental, 59
plants, 55
play, 7, 16, 53, 58
pleistocene, xii
poison, 56
political power, xiii
politics, 56
population, xiv, 1, 2, 3, 4, 7, 8, 11, 12, 13, 15, 16, 17, 18, 19, 21, 22, 23, 37, 54, 57, 59, 61
population size, xiv, 1, 4, 7, 8, 11, 12, 13, 16, 17, 18, 19, 21, 22, 54, 61
positive emotions, xii, 39, 50
power, xiii
preference, 4, 16, 17, 22, 37, 48, 49, 50, 52
press, xiv, 58
primates, 21, 22, 39, 51, 57
priming, 53
private, xi, 1, 3, 53
program, 56
property, vi
protection, xiii
protein, 61
psychology, 55
public, xiii, 1, 2, 7, 56

public interest, 56
public support, xiii
Puerto Rican, 15

Q

quail, 17, 49
quartile, 4

R

radiation, 55
rail, xi
random, 22
rat, 1, 41, 51
reconstruction, 55
recovery, xiii, 56, 60
Red List, xiii, 58
refugees, xii
regression, 22, 23, 24
regulations, 57
reintroduction, xi, xii, 53, 55, 58, 60
relationship, xiii, 11, 17, 22, 37, 39, 58, 61
relaxation, 8
reproduction, 7
reptiles, ix, xiii, xiv, 1, 3, 4, 5, 7, 8, 9, 11, 12, 22, 27, 48, 53, 54, 61
reservation, 59
resources, 60
rhino, xi
risks, 8, 11, 53, 58
rodents, 39
Royal Society, 57

S

sample, 5, 15
sand, 15
scarce resources, 60
services, vi
shape, 18, 50, 56
sheep, 1, 17, 60

short-term, 13
silver, 17
SIS, 1, 17
skills, 7
snakes, xii, 15, 21, 22, 23, 25, 39, 48, 58, 61
social construct, xiii
software, 60
source populations, xi
South America, iii
specific tax, 15
standards, xii
stimulus, 18
stochastic, 7, 8
strategies, ix
strength, 37
students, 2, 51
survival, xi, 13, 16, 53, 55, 58, 60

T

tamarin, xi, 51
taxa, ix, xii, xiii, xiv, 1, 2, 3, 7, 12, 15, 18, 21, 25, 26, 27, 28, 29, 30, 31, 32, 33, 34, 35, 36, 39, 42, 43, 44, 45, 46, 47, 53, 54
taxonomic, ix, xii, xiii, xiv, 2, 16, 23, 24, 61
taxonomy, 1, 60, 61
temperament, 59
threatened, ix, 11, 12, 13, 21
tiger, xiii
time, xi, 8, 53

tortoises, xiii, 16, 49
training, 7
traits, xiii, 48, 50, 51
tribal, xii
turtles, xiii, 2, 15, 16, 17, 21, 22, 27, 39, 49

U

uniform, 18, 50

V

values, 5, 7, 9
variability, 2, 21, 22
variation, xi, 7, 16, 17, 18, 22, 23, 24, 37, 39, 48
vertebrate classes, 5, 11
vertebrates, xiii, xiv, 3, 5, 21, 39, 53, 54
village, 50
visible, 12

W

welfare, xii
wildlife, 57
wisdom, 51
woodhen, xi
worm, 48